Reducing Disproportionate Representation of Culturally Diverse Students in Special and Gifted Education

Edited by
Alfredo J. Artiles
Grace Zamora-Durán

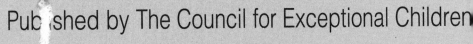
Published by The Council for Exceptional Children

Library of Congress Cataloging-in-Publication Data

Reducing disproportionate representation of culturally diverse
    students in special and gifted education / edited by Alfredo J.
    Artiles, Grace Zamora-Durán.
        p.   cm.
    Includes bibliographical references.
    ISBN 0-86586-297-4
    1. Special education–United States.   2. Minorities–Education–
United States.   3. Ability grouping in education–United States.
I. Artiles, Alfredo J.   II. Zamora-Durán, Grace.
LC3969.R43   1997
371.9'0973–dc21
                                                    97-17073
                                                    CIP

ISBN 0-86586-297-4

Copyright 1997 by The Council for Exceptional Children, 1920 Association
Drive, Reston, Virginia 20191-1589.

Stock No. P5219

Printed in the United States of America

10   9   8   7   6   5   4   3   2   1

Contents

1 Disproportionate Representation: A Contentious and Unresolved Predicament

Alfredo J. Artiles
University of California, Los Angeles

Grace Zamora-Durán
The Council for Exceptional Children

For decades, practitioners and researchers have debated about the disproportionate representation of culturally and linguistically diverse (CLD) students in special and gifted education programs (Dunn, 1968; Heller, Holtzman, & Messick, 1982). Implicit in these discussions is the notion that placement in special education programs is intrinsically harmful and enrollment in gifted education programs is highly desirable. However, not all educators agree with these assumptions, particularly because of the many factors and circumstances that influence student placement in these programs. Placement is indeed a complex problem that often elicits conflicting responses.

For instance, some special educators have argued that analyses of the disproportionate representation of CLD students need to transcend their focus on technical aspects and expand to include sociohistorical and political perspectives (Artiles & Trent, 1994). In addition, urban schools have been charged with misclassifying many CLD students, which raises questions about the special education assessment system (Gottlieb, Alter, Gottlieb, & Wishner, 1994). In contrast, others have questioned the basis of the proportionality debate: "But what is overrepresentation? If children grow up in an environment unfavorable to education –

The debate over the disproportionate representation of CLD students in special education programs goes to the heart of placement issues and societal attitudes surrounding these students' education.

Educators need to understand not only how exceptionality is defined but also how it is treated in current legal and educational systems.

or to the valuing of long-term goals or of compliance to adult demands – then why should we be surprised that more youngsters from such families would be in educational difficulty than their proportions in the society?" (Gallagher, 1994, p. 525).

This debate on placement, disproportionate representation, and misclassification is far from being resolved. Its far-reaching implications in special education include discussions about, among other topics, systemic reform and teacher education research (Artiles & Trent, in press; Lipsky & Gartner, 1996; Wang, 1995). Moreover, it is evident that at the root of these deliberations is a more profound issue, namely how individuals understand the very notion of human difference. Thus, educators need to grapple with the theoretical premises of the debate's arguments to unveil how human difference is construed in society. This will allow educators to understand not only how exceptionality is defined but also how it is treated in current legal and educational systems. In her seminal book, Martha Minow (1990) summarized the traditional approaches used to deal with the "dilemma of difference":

> The abnormal-persons approach converts the problem of legal treatment of persons into an either/or construction: a given individual should be treated like a normal person or else like an abnormal person. There are two, and only two, solutions, each defined in reference to the other.

> The rights approach enables advocates to challenge initial answers that otherwise would take this either/or form: asserting the rights of a disabled person, for example, can challenge the exclusion of that person from the community inhabited by "normal" people. Yet the rights approach still permits different treatment for those who are "really different" or who, in the minds of decision-makers, have traits that continue to distinguish them from the majority. In a sense, the rights approach also preserves the either/or construction of the problem: it allows people to move the line between the norm and the abnormal but maintains the idea of the distinction and its legal consequences. (pp. 214-215)

This brief discussion about the complexity of the disproportionality problem suggests that special educators need to address it from more sophisticated theoretical and empirical perspectives. Indeed, more research with CLD exceptional children is urgently needed (Gottlieb et al., 1994). Similarly, a theory of equal opportunity (Mithaug, 1996), a theory of disability/difference (Minow, 1990; Peters, 1993), and a theory of the decision-making processes of teachers and administrators – which takes into account interests, ideology, information, and institution (Weiss, 1995) – should be incorporated in future studies of disproportionate representation of CLD students.

From an applied perspective, the essence of the disproportional representation debate is the issue of inappropriate placement.

Purpose and Organization of the Book

It is beyond the scope of this book to provide an exhaustive discussion of the debate. Rather, this volume focuses on an important but neglected dimension of the debate, namely the need to address this problem from an applied perspective. In short, chapter authors are concerned with transcending the mere condemnation of this problem and with offering alternative strategies which practitioners can begin to test in their professional practice. Ultimately, efforts in this direction will contribute to adequately address the educational needs of all students.

From an applied perspective, the essence of the disproportional representation debate is the issue of inappropriate placement. Specifically, concern centers on the problem of false positives, that is, cases in which a CLD student is labeled disabled when in fact he or she is not and, thus, is inappropriately placed in a special education program. Likewise, overlooking the gifts and talents of CLD students and thereby omitting them from gifted education programs will prevent them from receiving the services that will contribute to the full development of their potential.

Although one of the first visible efforts to denounce the disproportionate representation issue was made over 25 years ago (Dunn, 1968), few efforts have been devoted to developing strategies that can be used in the daily routines of teachers. Indeed, little research and development monies have been allocated for such development, and virtually nobody has launched a systematic research program to grapple with this predicament. At the same time, as some continue to decry the disproportionate representation problem and to plead for more attention to it, practitioners have been left alone to struggle for solutions. Thus, it can be forcibly argued that research must be conducted which addresses this problem and which in turn will generate specific solutions for practitioners and parents. It was only a few years ago that the U.S. Department of Education funded a national center to address minority issues in special education, and much still remains to be done.

To aid in the search for solutions, The Council for Exceptional Children (CEC) convened in 1994 in San Diego the CEC Multicultural Symposium. A panel of researchers and educators assembled to ponder what is known and what could be done about disproportionate representation in special and gifted education programs. The session was well attended and highly interactive, and the presenters offered insightful analyses of the disproportionate representation problem. A tangible outcome of the session was an agreement to publish the presenters' papers. We grappled throughout the editorial process with the focus of and audience for this important project. Although the contributors had a great deal to share about the research base that informs efforts in this domain, we ultimately decided to focus on potential solutions that practitioners could use to improve their assessment, identification, and instructional practices with CLD students. The outcome of these efforts is this volume.

In Chapter 2, Robert Rueda addresses the important domain of instructional assessment. This is indeed a central task of teachers for it guides instructional planning and is used to monitor student learning. Rueda criticizes traditional standardized assessment approaches because they disregard students' prior knowledge and cultural backgrounds. He further argues that traditional approaches neglect to assess student learning in authentic, meaningful contexts. Rueda proposes the use of performance assessment approaches which address these limitations and allow teachers more flexibility in the design of assessment procedures.

In the next three chapters, contributors address three domains of student performance relevant to the analysis of disproportionate representation, namely, student behavior, language proficiency, and student ability — as expressed in students' talents and gifted performance. Sharon Ishii-Jordan's chapter (# 3) provides an insightful discussion about the culturally situated nature of student behavior. She suggests that educators need to be cognizant of the role of cultural meanings underlying human behavior when making decisions about what are normal and deviant behaviors and when making referrals to special education. Her discussion of these issues provides educators with ideas to better understand student behaviors as embedded in sociocultural contexts.

In turn, children's language proficiency is often a source of difficulties for teachers who work with students whose first language is not English. Prominent in this area is the issue of differential diagnosis. Specifically, teachers often wonder if a second-language learner's academic difficulties are due to his or her limited English proficiency or to a learning disability. In Chapter 4, Zamora-Durán and Reyes argue that educators need to be able to assess informally students' language proficiency to decide whether a more comprehensive assessment or a prereferral intervention is needed. They offer guidelines to examine students' language proficiency in the context of instructional conversations.

In Chapter 5, James Patton decries the underrepresentation of CLD students in gifted programs. He argues that this pattern is explained in part by the traditional overreliance on standardized intelligence tests to determine program eligibility. Patton proposes the use of a systematic and comprehensive system to screen and identify gifted and talented CLD students. He discusses several alternative assessment procedures as well as intervention models that can help CLD students to excel in these programs. More importantly, he argues that implicit in this new system is the need to redefine how ability and intelligence are understood and how professionals' beliefs and assumptions about CLD students and gifted performance must be transformed so the professionals they can fully appreciate the potential and contributions of this group of students. Chapter 6 presents a wrap-up and synthesis of the entire volume.

All in all, this book takes the perspective that teachers may engage in practices that contribute to disproportionate representation in special and gifted education programs of CLD students. Furthermore, current referral and assessment procedures exacerbate the problem. As stated earlier, this book does not address the many complicated issues related to disproportionate representation in these programs from theoretical or research perspectives. Rather, the goal is to provide solutions, or strategies, for practitioners to apply in their classrooms that can help reverse the trend of disproportionate representation.

Author Note

The first author wishes to acknowledge the support provided by a Faculty Career Development Award from the UCLA Chancellor's office during the preparation of this volume.

References

Artiles, A. J., & Trent, S .C. (1994). Overrepresentation of minority students in special education: A continuing debate. *The Journal of Special Education, 27,* 410-437.

Artiles, A. J., & Trent, S. C. (in press). Forging a research program on multicultural preservice teacher education: A proposed analytic scheme. In J. W. Lloyd, E. Kameenui, & D. Chard (Eds.), *Educating students with disabilities.* Hillsdale, NJ: Lawrence Erlbaum.

Dunn, L. M. (1968). Special education for the mildly retarded: Is much of it justifiable? *Exceptional Children, 23,* 5-21.

Gallagher, J. J. (1994). The pull of societal forces on special education. *The Journal of Special Education, 27,* 521-530.

Gottlieb, J., Alter, M., Gottlieb, B. W., & Wishner, J. (1994). Special education in urban America: It's not justifiable for many. *The Journal of Special Education, 27,* 453-465

Heller, K. A., Holtzman, W. H., & Messick, S. (1982). *Placing children in special education: A strategy for equity.* Washington, DC: National Academy Press.

Lipsky, D. K., & Gartner, A. (1996). Inclusion, school restructuring, and the remaking of American society. *Harvard Educational Review, 66,* 762-796.

Minow, M. (1990). *Making all the difference: Inclusion, exclusion, and American law.* Ithaca, NY: Cornell University Press.

Mithaug, D. E. (1996). *Equal opportunity theory.* Thousand Oaks, CA: Sage.

Peters, S. (1993). An ideological-cultural framework for the study of disability. In S. J. Peters (Ed.), *Education and disability in cross-cultural perspective* (pp. 19-37). New York: Garland.

Wang, M. C. (1995). Serving students with special needs: Equity and access. *Prospects, 25,* 287-297.

Weiss, C. H. (1995). The four "I's" of school reform: How interests, ideology, information, and institution affect teachers and principals. *Harvard Educational Review, 65,* 571-592.

2 Changing the Context of Assessment: The Move to Portfolios and Authentic Assessment

Robert Rueda
University of Southern California

Questions about the appropriate uses of assessment continue to represent an important issue for the field of special education. As an integral part of special education practice and service delivery, assessment has always been a central concern for special educators. It is the main tool through which access to services is provided and through which progress based on those services is evaluated for a variety of formal and informal purposes. Few would argue with the idea that assessment is especially critical for special education as it currently functions in public school settings.

In spite of its importance to special education, assessment has often been problematic, in particular for culturally and linguistically diverse (CLD) students

In spite of its importance to special education, assessment has often been problematic, in particular for culturally and linguistically diverse (CLD) students (Figueroa, 1990; Gersten & Woodward, 1994; Valdés & Figueroa, 1994). One reason for concern has been the charge that traditional standardized tests of ability tend to underestimate the ability and potential of some students. In addition, inappropriate measures and procedures have often been seen as the prime reason for inaccurate and stigmatizing labels as well as disproportionate representation in various special education categories.

One common characteristic of these traditional measures is that academic tasks can be presented in a compact, "objective," standard, easy-to-score-and-interpret format (Howell & Rueda, 1996). In general, these tests are designed to be "transportable" across a wide range of educational settings.

In the past, the overwhelming focus of efforts by special educators to address assessment-related concerns centered on ways to make the sorting and ranking of students more accurate. That is, a great deal of effort was spent in trying to ensure that a student had the "correct" label or had not been labeled in error.

Although these types of measures often provide a relatively quick and easy way to assess students, it is these very characteristics which have led to their disfavor among many in the educational community, especially in the assessment of children's language and literacy development (Anthony, Johnson, Mickelson, & Preece, 1991). Primary among the criticisms is that these tests normally do not accurately reflect real-world or authentic classroom tasks and demands. Moreover, they are criticized for only providing summary scores which are not useful in designing specific instruction and for allowing little or no adaptation to local classroom contexts (Shepard, 1989).

Concern about the use or misuse of traditional standardized tests and test data with language- and ethnic-minority children continues (Figueroa, 1989; Gifford, 1989; Miller-Jones, 1989; Rothman, 1992). The often narrow range of content, response formats, and sensitivity to students' test-taking and background knowledge have led to especially heated criticism with respect to language- and ethnic-minority students (Garcia & Pearson, 1991, 1994; Mercado & Romero, 1993). In short, many claim that traditional assessment removes cognition and problem-solving from authentic purposes and uses, tests arbitrary and esoteric skills in isolation, ignores individual students' prior knowledge and motivation, and therefore violates the principles of cognitive development as currently understood (Forman, Minick, & Stone, 1993; Marshall, 1992; Miller-Jones, 1989; Moll, 1990).

In the past, the overwhelming focus of efforts by special educators to address these assessment-related concerns for language- and ethnic-minority students centered on ways to make the sorting and ranking of students more accurate. That is, a great deal of effort was spent in trying to ensure that a student had the "correct" label or had not been labeled in error.

Clearly, a concern for equity has been at the center of much of the past discussion of assessment practices. Recently, a number of changes have occurred in the larger context in which assessment is carried out which has served to broaden the discussion. These changes have helped stimulate questions about the very nature and role of assessment both in and outside of special education over and above the issue of sorting and ranking.

One result of these questions has been the increasing adoption of newer forms of assessment such as performance-based and related authentic measures. This chapter first highlights some of the issues related to the adoption and use of these measures with CLD children, especially in light of changes in how development and learning are viewed. The remainder of this chapter details some of these changes and then describes characteristics of these alternative measures and the issues surrounding their use in the context of linguistic and cultural diversity. Finally, some of the implications for practice will be discussed, including issues related to disproportionate representation.

More recent conceptions of literacy define it as a process of constructing meaning, relating new knowledge to prior knowledge, developing personal responses, and applying knowledge to real problems and situations.

Changes in Views of Learning and Cognitive Development

While IQ tests remain at the heart of assessment for special education placement, there have been significant developments in how researchers and theorists conceptualize the processes underlying learning and in what tests should measure. Until about the 1960s, a behaviorist and to a lesser extent a Piagetian approach were highly influential in conceptualizing learning processes and influencing school practice. While the format and content of traditional standardized tests were not entirely compatible with Piaget's emphasis on how children construct meaning, they were much more compatible with a behavioral orientation. However, more recently, information processing and, increasingly, sociocultural perspectives have come to the forefront in both research and practice (Byrnes, 1996).

These theoretical developments regarding learning and cognitive development have been reflected in academic settings where basic language and literacy are the primary concern. In the past, for example, literacy (especially in remedial settings) was seen primarily as mastery or assessment of discrete, unconnected skills often in a fixed, hierarchical sequence. Now, the underlying cognitive processes involved in literacy are increasingly emphasized. More recent conceptions of literacy define it as a process of constructing meaning, relating new knowledge to prior knowledge, developing personal responses, and applying knowledge to real problems and situations (Rhodes & Dudley-Marling, 1988).

Students' "funds of knowledge" – the knowledge and skills they and their families use to navigate daily life – have been found to be especially critical resources in language and literacy learning for CLD students

In addition, the "situated" nature of cognition and the impact of context on cognitive processes is increasingly acknowledged. Consistent with a sociocultural approach to learning and cognitive development (Moll, 1990), literacy is viewed not so much as a collection of skills but as social and cultural practices that vary across cultures, communities, and contexts even within the same setting (Heap, 1989; Hiebert, 1991; Santa Barbara Classroom Discourse Group, 1992; Walsh, 1991). Moreover, although schools tend to exclusively value traditional "reading and writing" in formal academic tasks (Bloom & Green, 1992), a great many literate activities and practices occur in everyday settings and are typically not considered or valued (Barton, 1991; Gee, 1991; Heath, 1983; Robinson, 1987).

These developing theories of cognitive development and learning have also had an impact on language development and instruction in schools. For a long time, little was known about the cognitive processes involved in how children acquire and use more than one language, which factors promote proficiency and fluency, or how the development of first and second language and literacy impact each other or cognitive development in general. Most often, speaking more than one language was seen as detrimental for cognitive development and learning and an obstacle in acquiring English. However, a great deal more information is now available regarding bilingualism and language acquisition (Genesee, 1994; McLeod, 1994).

The importance of primary language as a cognitive tool and as a basis for complex learning and for second language acquisition is now recognized as critical. Factors which promote language acquisition such as additive learning environments and meaningful communicative contexts are seen as critical for both first and second language. Students' "funds of knowledge" – the knowledge and skills they and their families use to navigate daily life – have been found to be especially critical resources in language and literacy learning for CLD students (Moll, 1990).

These evolving views of learning and cognitive development have made less clear the connection between theory and traditional measurement, especially IQ tests. As just noted, contemporary cognitive theory increasingly emphasizes the impact of culture, context, and social interaction on learning and assessment (Hollins, King, & Hayman, 1994; Marshall, 1992; Moll, 1990). These recent theories about learning and development place a great deal of importance for self-regulated learners on aspects of higher order thinking, problem-solving, cooperative cognitive activity, mediation, self-monitoring, and strategic behavior. Yet, these qualities are difficult to tap with traditional assessment methods, and often there is not a good match between assessment practices and tools and the changes in knowledge briefly described earlier.

In the past, traditional IQ tests were part of a process focusing on hypothesized deficits of CLD students as an explanation for low achievement, often resulting in special education placement and disproportionate representation. More recently, many authors have begun to challenge the practice of blaming low achievement solely on low IQ either alone or in combination with children's primary language and culture (Trueba, 1989). The search for deficits is now more balanced by attempts to document the cultural, linguistic, and social resources (funds of knowledge) students and their families bring to school and to see how these can be used in academic tasks and problem-solving activities (Moll, 1990) Taken together, these factors define a context for assessment quite different from what existed previously.

These new forms focus on learning processes as opposed to only final products; on tasks requiring construction of meaning on complex tasks rather than recall of discrete bits of information; on tasks which take place over time rather than on a one-time basis; and on activities connected to higher order thinking as opposed to rote learning only.

The Move to Portfolios and Authentic Assessment

It is clear that in many ways traditional testing practices fall short with respect to current research and theory. Concern is increasing about (a) the mismatch between the traditional formats and content of tests and the current knowledge base on effective classroom learning activities and environments (Garcia & Pearson, 1994) and (b) the usefulness of standardized scores or other traditional data for informing teachers in their day-to-day classroom practice (Darling-Hammond, Ancess, & Falk, 1995).

One interesting result is the move to develop new forms of assessment. These new forms focus on learning processes as opposed to only final products; on tasks requiring construction of meaning on complex tasks rather than recall of discrete bits of

Performance-based assessment is especially critical for special educators in light of the traditional and central role that assessment has played in special education practice.

information; on tasks which take place over time rather than on a one-time basis; and on activities connected to higher order thinking as opposed to rote learning only. Especially prominent in the discussion about the shortcomings of traditional assessment practices is the call for more authentic, performance-based assessment (Hiebert, Afflerback, & Valencia, 1994). This has led to increasing use of alternative assessments such as holistic evaluation of work products, increased use of actual classroom work products and tasks, use of scoring rubrics for judging these academic products, and portfolios.

These developments are especially critical for special educators in light of the traditional and central role that assessment has played in special education practice. The move toward performance-based measures has been strongly advocated not only for mainstream students (Anthony, Johnson, Mickelson, & Preece, 1991; Calfee & Perfumo, 1993) but also, and particularly, for language-minority students (Garcia & Pearson, 1994). Because these types of measures are significantly different from many of those traditionally relied on in special education practice, some of their characteristics and some of the issues related to their use are described next.

In general, performance-based assessment refers to assessment relying on real-world tasks and often involving evaluation of performance through rubrics or benchmarks that identify characteristics of exemplary performance, acceptable performance, or unacceptable performance. In literacy, for example, a traditional test might require students to answer multiple-choice questions, fill in blanks, or provide short answers to comprehension questions on a text segment. In contrast, literacy performance-assessment tasks might include observation of a student as he or she progresses through the various phases of the writing process to the completion and publication of a final piece. Within the context of this activity, competence in drafting, revising, story mapping, and other relevant aspects of performance might be focused on in addition to the quality of the final product.

Harrington-Lueker (1991) has described performance assessment as "the umbrella term for a variety of measures – including essays, portfolios, projects, and videotapes – that test the so-called higher order thinking skills many believe are beyond the reach of multiple-choice items" (p. 20). According to Kennedy (1992) and Lin, Baker, and Dunbar (1991), common features of these types of assessments include complex learning; higher order thinking; authenticity (inherent value to the students); stimulation of a wide variety of active responses of students; tasks requiring multiple steps; and significant commitments of student time and effort.

Rather than being asked to merely regurgitate knowledge on a test, students are required to use higher mental processes (e.g., thinking, cognition, perception, creativity) that relate to the "real world" in ways that have not traditionally been tapped. The primary benefit of performance assessment is that students do complex, real-world tasks that are engaging (have an authentic purpose) and seamless with instruction (Linn et al., 1991).

Under the umbrella of performance assessment is a growing practice which has come to be known as portfolio assessment. Valencia (in press) defines portfolios as "a purposeful collection of student work and records of progress and achievement collected over time" (p. 3). As some have noted, portfolios are common in fields outside of education, for example, for artists, photographers, and models. In these contexts, portfolios serve as tangible evidence of accomplishments and document skill growth over time. By definition, they are not rigidly structured in terms of content or format and, thus, can reflect a variety of activities and products. In addition, teachers and others can use portfolios as the basis for collecting and examining effort, improvement, developmental processes, and achievement as well as for meeting the accountability demands usually achieved by more formal testing procedures.

There are several types of portfolios:

Student portfolios inform the student and document student self-reflection.

Working portfolios are designed for the teacher's daily use and as a primary tool for developing and modifying instruction on a short-term basis.

Showcase portfolios inform the parents and surrounding educational community.

Cumulative portfolios are designed for accountability and evaluative purposes.

1. *Student portfolios* inform the student and document student self-reflection.

2. *Working portfolios* are designed for the teacher's daily use and as a primary tool for developing and modifying instruction on a short-term basis.

3. *Showcase portfolios* inform the parents and surrounding educational community.

4. *Cumulative portfolios* are designed for accountability and evaluative purposes.

A critical difference among these types of portfolios is the degree to which they represent high-stakes or low-stakes testing (Madaus, 1987). Briefly, high-stakes testing is assessment that pupils, teachers, or administrators perceive as likely to have life or career consequences such as grade promotion, graduation, or merit pay for teachers. In contrast, low-stakes assessment is normally devoid of such perceived consequences, as when a state merely provides test data to districts so they can diagnose or fix their own problems as they see fit or when data are used to monitor and inform day-to-day instructional activities. In this latter instance, testing may be considered high or low stakes depending upon the local context.

Effective Use of Portfolios

Researchers who have investigated teachers' use of performance assessment in the classroom (Stiggins & Bridgeford, 1985; Stiggins & Conklin, 1992) indicate that, although a large number of teachers do use it, over two-thirds are not comfortable about the quality of the assessments they carry out (Stiggins & Bridgeford, 1985). Moreover, many teachers recognize that, in spite of the fact that more authentic measures are being used, their lack of formal training in classroom assessment (traditional paper-and-pencil as well performance assessments) may lead them to assess poorly (Gullickson, 1986; Schafer & Lissitz, 1987). These and other studies provide a basis for improving the use of portfolios in everyday practice. In addition, Stiggins & Bridgeford (1985) found that many factors which impact validity and reliability are not attended to in everyday classroom situations. Other investigators (Garcia, Rasmussen, Stobbe, & Garcia, 1990; Paratore, Shoemaker, Mauro, & Matrinko, 1996; Rueda & Garcia, in press) have examined portfolio use in culturally and linguistically diverse settings.

Taken together, the findings from these studies provide a basis for improving the use of portfolios. The findings include

- Inform pupils before assessment takes place of what constitutes a good performance.

- Plan scoring or rating procedures prior to assessment.

- Think carefully prior to assessment about which level of pupil performance would be considered adequate.

- Where possible, plan assessment around multiple rather than single observations.

- Keep records so that the evaluation of individual performance is not based on memory alone.

- Avoid portfolios as a tool for "going through the motions," but rather use them to shape instructional decisions especially for the lowest performing students.

- Use portfolios to help shift responsibility from the teacher to the students.

- Realize that there may sometimes be a conflict between the data being collected from portfolio assessments and the traditional data valued by administrators.

- Although there may be an initial struggle to find ways to collect and manage data in view of scarce time and resources, most teachers successfully integrate portfolios into their classrooms.

- Portfolios should be seen as an important instructional tool. There is some evidence that portfolio data can lead to more numerous, more specific, and more detailed recommendations and judgments about students than traditional tests.

- Portfolios are especially useful in identifying strengths of students rather than only deficits.

- Portfolios are not neutral tools. How one uses portfolio data is filtered by basic beliefs about general issues such as learning or specific issues such as bilingualism or literacy. These underlying beliefs, perspectives, and assumptions are important influences on the use of portfolio and other performance-based assessment practices.

The following section will examine some suggestions for how performance-based and portfolio assessment can be integrated into practice, given what is known about continuing problems with disproportionate representation of CLD children in special education; about developments in the theories of learning, cultural diversity, and second-language acquisition; and about the shortcomings of traditional assessment.

It is increasingly clear that all students bring significant knowledge and resources to school. In the past, where these did not exactly match the knowledge of the classroom, they were often dismissed as unimportant or even treated as deficits to overcome. However, these have been shown to be extremely valuable resources in both curriculum development and instruction.

Using Portfolios in Diverse Settings

As Support for Primary Language Instruction

Much of the recent work with English learners suggests the importance of the primary language as a foundation for English language and literacy, as well as for more complex academic tasks. One of the primary weaknesses of standardized tests, in this regard, is that they are often highly sensitive to language-related factors and often mask the competence of students that might otherwise be apparent. On the other hand, portfolios can accommodate language differences much more readily. Wherever possible, they should be used to document and support primary language instruction. When collected over time, portfolios can also be used to document the interplay between first and second language acquisition.

As Documentation for Funds of Knowledge

It is increasingly clear that all students bring significant knowledge and resources to school. In the past, where these did not exactly match the knowledge of the classroom, they were often dismissed as unimportant or even treated as deficits to overcome. However, these have been shown to be extremely valuable resources in both curriculum development and instruction. Portfolios represent a valuable way of documenting the nature of these funds of knowledge and their use in classroom activities. The use of these funds of knowledge might be found in students' writing, for example, or in personal responses to various types of text.

As a Reflective Tool

One neglected aspect of portfolio use is that it does not simply represent an alternative assessment tool. Rather, the fundamental beliefs and assumptions about teaching and learning that are implicit in the use of portfolios differ significantly from those that underlie traditional instruction (Poplin, 1988). There is some evidence that these beliefs are so deeply held that they are often difficult to access and even more difficult to reflect on and change. Fortunately, portfolios offer a useful tool for reflecting on one's practice, especially the working portfolio described earlier. Portfolios can be used to document the nature of activities that students are being asked to engage in, to examine the assumptions and beliefs that underlie various activities, and to compare students' performances under different learning conditions. Moreover, they can serve a similar function for students in reflecting not only on their own learning but on themselves as learners.

As Support for High Level, Complex Problem-Solving

Traditional tests have often been criticized for trivializing learning. This is because some traditional testing formats take knowledge out of the context of learning and examine it independently of how and where it was acquired. One unfortunate consequence is that sometimes this results in assessments which emphasize rote knowledge or small bits of unconnected knowledge. However, one feature of performance assessments and portfolios is that they can be built around normally occurring classroom tasks and can be used to document learning processes as children engage in whole, meaningful, problem-solving activities and projects. When used to document the cognitive, linguistic, and learning processes which occur in these learning contexts, portfolios support the complex, meaningful learning which is increasingly valued as an outcome of schooling.

To Show You Are Making a Difference

As noted earlier, assessment has been central to the field of special education. In the case of CLD students, most often it has been discussed in the context of categorization or placement especially because of issues related to disproportionate representation. In past efforts to address both this problem and the accompanying misdiagnosis, it was often assumed that once a student was in the "correct" placement or had the "correct" label or even was decertified, he or she would progress satisfactorily. However, it is increasingly recognized that more important than monitoring the label or placement is the actual academic gains realized by the child. In view of this concern with monitoring outcomes and striving for not just equal opportunity but equal outcomes, the role of assessment has begun to shift to its use as a tool to document academic outcomes.

One feature of performance assessments and portfolios is that they can be built around normally occurring classroom tasks and can be used to document learning processes as children engage in whole, meaningful, problem-solving activities and projects.

Because performance measures are often grounded in actual classroom work, they are more accessible to teachers, parents, and students.

Because performance measures are often grounded in actual classroom work, they are more accessible to teachers, parents, and students. Cumulative portfolios are especially valuable because, unlike standardized measures, they provide snapshots of progress over time.

To Inform Parents and the Larger Community

Perhaps because of its early ties to the medical profession, special education has not historically placed great emphasis on the role of family and the larger community. Fortunately, the important role they play is now recognized as critical in all phases of the educational process, especially for students who are less acculturated or who are in the process of mastering English. Here again, portfolios can serve a valuable function in this enhanced view of teaching and learning. Showcase portfolios provide a useful tool for documenting academic achievement for external audiences not only for an individual child but for an entire class or school.

Cautions Regarding Portfolios

The gradual but growing incorporation of these new assessment methods into many classrooms, both in regular and special education, raises many interesting issues and questions. As noted earlier, there has been continuing concern about the misuse of tests and test data with CLD students (Figueroa, 1989; Gifford, 1989; Miller-Jones, 1989; Rothman, 1992), especially with regard to misdiagnosis and placement in special and remedial tracks (Figueroa, 1990; Valdés & Figueroa, 1994; Valencia, 1991).

Because they do not have many of the limitations of some standardized measures, portfolios and other authentic measures have often been seen as a way of addressing this problem. It has usually been assumed that by their very nature – especially the fact that they are grounded in actual classroom-based tasks – portfolios and other authentic measures reduce the bias which has often been the target of criticism with more traditional measures. There are several issues which need to be considered in this regard.

Does the Use of Portfolios Eliminate Bias?

There remain questions as to whether the assumption of the bias-free nature of portfolios and their use is warranted (Nettles & Nettles, 1995). For example, if portfolios are showcase or cumulative portfolios, they are normally judged according to some preestablished benchmarks or standards by raters. The same bias which may affect other facets of the special education system might be expected to have an impact here as well. Raters might be unfamiliar with nonstandard English, for example, and emphasize that aspect of a child's written work to the exclusion of the more critical reasoning, thought processes, and communicative intent. Likewise, if a teacher does not view a child's primary language as valuable or as an instructional resource, the adoption of portfolio assessment will do nothing to change those beliefs.

Conflicts Between Beliefs and Practice

Another potential problem with portfolios and authentic assessment is that they are based on a particular view of teaching and learning which may not be evident in all classrooms. If a teacher's views and beliefs regarding teaching and learning are significantly different that those which underlie these new assessment practices, how will he or she reconcile the two? How does portfolio assessment get integrated into classrooms dominated by traditional transmission-oriented instructional practices? Unless a clear match exists between what is guiding instruction and what is guiding assessment, the portfolio may become nothing more than a repository for examples of the same traditional practices which in the past have led to underestimating the competence of some students.

Managing Time and Resources

Another issue has to do with management. Clearly, these types of assessments require more focused observation of individual students over time as well as possible changes in normal routines. How do teachers incorporate these new practices into their established routines? Although many teachers manage to do this successfully, it does involve some rethinking of the teacher's time and perhaps reorganizing of classroom activities and even physical set-

Unless a clear match exists between what is guiding instruction and what is guiding assessment, the portfolio may become nothing more than a repository for examples of the same traditional practices which in the past have led to underestimating the competence of some students.

ting. Many teachers address this problem by emphasizing cooperative work groups and centers where students can work independently, by teaching students to help collect and assess their own learning and work products, and other means. If this factor is not considered, it is possible and even likely that portfolios will be seen as too burdensome for teachers and district administrators to implement especially when compared to traditional assessment.

Conflicting Purposes for Assessment

In spite of the seeming benefits of performance-based assessment, some larger policy issues with particular implications for the field of special education need to be considered. For example, how do (or should) classroom portfolios correspond with the traditional functions of standardized tests such as sorting and comparing students – functions that continue to be central for defining eligibility for special education services? How can assessment outcomes be compared (e.g., across classrooms) when they may be collected across very different classroom contexts? If classrooms and activities are authentic, almost by definition there will be wide variance across classrooms. How do these measures meet the demand for large-scale accountability which is currently being asked of the educational system? Should portfolios be compared to standards or benchmarks developed at the individual, classroom, school, district, state, or national levels? Do the data produced by these new measures lead to different decisions about students than traditional measures? That is, does portfolio assessment result in a more fair and accurate picture of language- and ethnic-minority students than other types of assessment?

The answers to these questions cannot be resolved unequivocally. However, it is clear that there are problems with the tools and practices which have dominated the field for most of its history, and it is imperative that promising alternatives be explored.

Conclusion

As indicated earlier, current understandings of literacy, language development, and learning are significantly different from those of the recent past. This changing context has led to a search for new ways to assess growth in these areas. The shift to new ways of assessing learning is further driven by continuing concerns for equity and the view that traditional, especially standardized, approaches to assessment result in biased data. Portfolio assessment is commonly mentioned as an alternative that can address these concerns and consequently is being adopted by more and more school districts. Many educators regard it as an especially attractive alternative in the assessment of language- and ethnic-minority students.

However, although portfolio assessment is quickly being adopted in both special and regular education settings for these reasons, the previous discussion suggests that several important issues still require consideration. For example, the transition from traditional to more authentic types of assessment needs to be seen as more than a simple replacement of one technique with another. Consideration must be given to practitioners' beliefs and assumptions and the overall social context in the individual classroom where assessment takes place. The "paradigm wars" which permeate many of the current journals suggest the importance of attending to these beliefs and assumptions, especially in areas such as professional development. It also means that time and resources to reflect on these issues must be an important part of the design of ongoing professional development as well as everyday practice (Cambourne & Turbill, 1994; Ruiz, Rueda, Figueroa, & Boothroyd, 1995). Sadly, this is not a common feature in the lives of most teachers, especially in these times of shrinking resources and expanding challenges to public education.

As some of the research described earlier suggests, portfolios may in fact lead to different evaluations of students than those based on more traditional data. This is especially encouraging for those concerned with past inequities for linguistically and culturally diverse students in special education. Although authentic and performance-based assessment and portfolios represent potentially powerful alternative tools in assessing learning, especially with English learners, their usefulness depends on how and why they are used by individual teachers. If they are superimposed on curricula in which students have little opportunity to engage in collaboration, complex problem-solving, and authentic tasks, the power of the approach will be lost.

The transition from traditional to more authentic types of assessment needs to be seen as more than a simple replacement of one technique with another. Consideration must be given to practitioners' beliefs and assumptions and the overall social context in the individual classroom where assessment takes place.

In sum, these alternative procedures will not automatically lead to better quality data and more favorable circumstances for students: Existing beliefs and perspectives need to be considered as well as their influence on the structure of day-to-day classroom activities. There is a great need to examine how effective teachers are using portfolios, which theoretical and applied issues are being raised by these uses, and how the answers to these questions can ensure better outcomes for students which is, after all, the ultimate indicator of success.

Author Note

This work was prepared with partial support from the Office of Educational Research and Improvement (OERI) of the U.S. Department of Education, under Cooperative Agreement No. R117G10022. The findings and opinions expressed here are those of the author and do not necessarily reflect the positions or policies of OERI. The author would like to express appreciation to all the teachers who gave their valuable time in that part of the author's work reported here.

References

Anthony, R. J., Johnson, T. D., Mickelson, N. I., & Preece, A. (1991). *Evaluating literacy: A perspective for change.* Portsmouth, NH: Heinemann.

Barton, D. (1991). The social nature of writing. In D. Barton & R. Ivanic (Eds.), *Writing in the community* (pp. 1-13). Newbury Park, CA: Sage.

Bloom, D., & Green, J. L. (1992). Educational contexts of literacy. *Annual Review of Applied Linguistics, 12,* 49-70.1

Byrnes, J. P. (1996). *Cognitive development and learning in instructional contexts.* Boston: Allyn & Bacon.

Calfee, R. C., & Perfumo, P. (1993). Student portfolios: Opportunities for a revolution in assessment. *Journal of Reading, 36*(7), 532-537.

Cambourne, B., & Turbill, J. (1994). *Responsive evaluation: Making valid judgements about student literacy.* Portsmouth, NH: Heinemann.

Darling-Hammond, L., Ancess, J., & Falk, B. (1995). *Authentic assessment in action: Studies of schools and students at work.* New York: Teachers College Press.

Figueroa, R. (1989). Psychological testing of linguistic-minority students: Knowledge gaps and regulations. *Exceptional Children, 56,* 145-152.

Figueroa, R. (1990). Assessment of linguistic minority group children. In C. R. Reynolds & R. W. Kamphaus (Eds.), *Handbook of psychological and educational research: Intelligence and achievement* (pp. 671-696). New York: Guilford Press.

Forman, E. A., Minick, N., & Stone, C. A. (1993). *Contexts for learning: Sociocultural dynamics in children's development.* New York: Oxford University Press.

Garcia, G. E., & Pearson, P. D. (1991). The role of assessment in a diverse society. In E. H. Hiebert (Ed.), *Literacy in a diverse society: Perspectives, practices, and policies* (pp. 253-278). New York: Teachers College Press.

Garcia, G. E., & Pearson, P. D. (1994). Assessment and diversity. In L. Darling Hammond (Ed.), *Review of research in education* (vol. 20, pp. 337-391). Washington, DC: American Educational Research Association.

Garcia, E., Rasmussen, B., Stobbe, C., & Garcia, E. (1990). Portfolios: An assessment tool in support of instruction. *International Journal of Educational Research, 14*(5), 431-436.

Gee, J. (1991). *Social linguistics and literacies: Ideology in discourse.* London: Falmer Press.

Genesee, F. (Ed.). (1994). *Educating second language children: The whole child, the whole curriculum, the whole community.* Cambridge, England: Cambridge University Press.

Gersten, R., & Woodward, J. (1994). The language-minority student and special education: Issues, trends, and paradoxes. *Exceptional Children, 60,* 310-322.

Gifford, B. R. (Ed.). (1989). *Test policy and the politics of opportunity allocation: The workplace and the law.* Boston: Kluwer Academic Publishers.

Gullickson, A. R. (1986). Teacher education and teacher-perceived needs in educational measurement and evaluation. *Journal of Educational Measurement, 23*(4), 327-354.

Harrington-Lueker, D. (1991). Beyond multiple choice: The push to assess performance. *Executive Educator, 13,* 20-22.

Heap, J. L. (1989). Sociality and cognition in collaborative computer writing. In D. Bloom (Ed.), *Classrooms and literacy* (pp. 135-157). Norwood, NJ: Ablex.

Heath, S. (1983). *Ways with words.* New York: Cambridge University Press.

Hiebert, E. H. (1991). *Literacy for a diverse society: Perspectives, practices, and policies.* New York: Teachers College Press.

Hiebert, E., Afflerback, P., & Valencia, S. (Eds.). (1994). *Authentic reading assessment: Practices and possibilities.* Newark, DE: International Reading Association.

Hollins, E. R., King, J. E., & Hayman, W. C. (1994). *Teaching diverse populations: Formulating a knowledge base.* Albany, NY: State University of New York Press.

Howell, K., & Rueda, R. (1996). Achievement testing with culturally and linguistically diverse students. In L. A. Suzuki, P. J. Meller, & J. G. Ponterotto (Eds.), *Handbook of multicultural assessment: Clinical, psychological, and educational applications.* (pp. 253-290). San Francisco: Jossey Bass.

Kennedy, R. (1992). What is performance assessment? *New Directions for Education Reform, 1*(2), 21-27.

Linn, R. L., Baker, E. L., & Dunbar, S. B. (1991). Complex, performance-based assessment: Expectations and validation criteria. *Educational Researcher, 20*(8), 15-21.

Madaus, G. (1987). *Testing and the curriculum.* Chestnut Hill, MA: Boston College.

Marshall, H. H. (Ed.). (1992). *Redefining student learning: Roots of educational change.* Norwood, NJ: Ablex Publishing.

McLeod, B. (Ed.). (1994). *Language and learning: Educating linguistically diverse students.* Albany, NY: State University of New York Press.

Mercado, C., & Romero, M. (1993). Assessment of students in bilingual education. In M. B. Arias & U. Cassanova (Eds.), *Ninety-second yearbook of the National Society for the Study of Education, Part II. Bilingual education: Politics, practice, and research* (pp. 144-169). Chicago: University of Chicago Press.

Miller-Jones, D. (1989). Culture and testing. *American Psychologist, 44*(2), 360-366.

Moll, L. C. (Ed.). (1990). *Vygotsky and education: Instructional implications and applications of sociohistorical psychology.* New York: Cambridge University Press.

Nettles, M. T. & Nettles, A. L. (Eds.). (1995). *Equity and excellence in educational testing and assessment.* Boston: Kluwer Academic Publishers.

Paratore, J. R., Shoemaker, S., Mauro, A., & Matrinko, D. (1996). Documenting children's literacy: Learning from classroom teachers about implementing literacy portfolios. In L. R. Putnam (Ed), *How to become a better reading teacher: Strategies for assessment and intervention* (pp. 123-139). Englewood Cliffs, NJ: Merrill.

Poplin, M. S. (1988). Holistic/constructivist principles of the teaching/learning process: Implications for the field of learning disabilities. *Journal of Learning Disabilities, 21*(7), 401-416.

Rhodes, L. K, & Dudley-Marling, C. (1988). *Readers and writers with a difference: A holistic approach to teaching learning disabled students.* Portsmouth, NH: Heinemann.

Robinson, J. L. (1987). Literacy in society: Readers and writers in the worlds of discourse. In D. Bloom (Ed.), *Literacy and schooling* (pp. 327-353). Norwood, NJ: Ablex.

Rothman, R. (1992, October 21). Study confirms fears regarding commercial tests. *Education Week, 12*(7), pp. 1, 13.

Rueda, R., & Garcia, E. (in press). Do portfolios make a difference for diverse students? The influence of type of data on making instructional decisions. *Learning Disabilities Research and Practice.*

Ruiz, N. T., Rueda, R., Figueroa, R. A., & Boothroyd, M. (1995). Shifting paradigms of bilingual special education teachers: Complex responses to educational reform. *Journal of Learning Disabilities, 28*(10), 622-635.

Santa Barbara Classroom Discourse Group. (1992). Constructing literacy in classrooms: Literate actions as social accomplishment. In H. Marshall (Ed.), *Redefining student learning* (p. 119-150). Norwood, NJ: Ablex.

Schafer, W. D., & Lissitz, R. W. (1987). Measurement training for school personnel: Recommendations and reality. *Journal of Teacher Education, 38*(3), 57-63.

Shepard, L. A. (1989). Why we need better assessments. *Educational Leadership, 46,*(7), 4-9.

Stiggins, R. A., & Bridgeford, N. J. (1985). The ecology of classroom assessment. *Journal of Educational Measurement, 22*(4), 271-286.

Stiggins, R. A., & Conklin, N. F. (1992). *In teacher's hands.* Albany, NY: State University of New York Press.

Trueba, H. T. (1989). *Raising silent voices: Educating the linguistic minorities in the 21st century.* New York: Newbury House.

Valdés, G., & Figueroa, R. A. (1994). *Bilingualism and testing: A special case of bias.* Norwood, NJ: Ablex Publishing.

Valencia, R. (1991). *Chicano academic underachievement: Research and public policy agendas for the 1990's.* London: Falmer Press.

Valencia, S. W. (in press). Portfolios: Panacea or Pandora's box. In F. Finch (Ed.), *Educational performance testing.* Chicago: Riverside Publishing.

Walsh, C. (1991). *Literacy as praxis: Culture, language, and pedagogy.* Norwood, NJ: Ablex.

3 When Behavior Differences Are Not Disorders

Sharon R. Ishii-Jordan
University of Nebraska-Lincoln

With entire educational systems currently being restructured to match how and why schools deliver formal education, it becomes quite evident that special education must also receive its turn under the magnifying lens. Revised conceptualizations in special education have grown out of numerous debates relative to general education restructuring, special education program or product outcomes, special education costs, and political effects on educational policies. Unfortunately, those conceptualizations generally view students with learning, behavioral, or sensory disabilities as an aggregate. Consideration is not given to such complicating factors as the impact of cultural and linguistic diversity on both students and educational restructuring designs.

This chapter will provide some thoughts on the critical issues that impact children with cultural and linguistic differences (CLD) who exhibit behaviors that are viewed as disordered.

As new ideas of service delivery for students with disabilities are bandied about, and even implemented, the category of *serious emotional disorder* is not one likely to be considered in the same breath as other disability categories in debates over special education change. Regular educators do not relish working with this population of students in their classrooms (Johnson, 1987), and advocates for this population are among the smallest in representative numbers. This chapter will provide some thoughts on the critical issues that impact children with cultural and linguistic differences (CLD) who exhibit behaviors that are viewed as disordered. Specifically, the chapter will focus on concerns with defining behavioral disorders, assessing emotional/behavioral disorders (EBD), intervening with the student, and training the professionals involved with the student.

Humans learn to behave through their cultural references and expectations. Because of that, all the behaviors exhibited by an individual reflect the experiences encountered in his or her life. Furthermore, the aggregate of one's experiences defines one's culture. The more experiences an individual has, the more his or her own culture changes from that of the initial natal environment.

Behavior as a Culturally Based Phenomenon

To understand how students are identified for EBD services, it is important to first understand how behavior is viewed differently across cultures. Behavior is culture related. Humans learn to behave through their cultural references and expectations. Because of that, all the behaviors exhibited by an individual reflect the experiences encountered in his or her life. Furthermore, the *aggregate* of one's experiences defines one's culture. The more experiences an individual has, the more his or her own culture changes from that of the initial natal environment. It follows, then, that one interprets the behaviors of others based on one's own cultural meanings. The diversity of experiences within and among cultural groups almost defies any broad generalizations; however, certain themes or characteristics have been fairly consistent among certain racial or ethnic groups. There is a greater likelihood that general characteristics will be exhibited by individuals if they are more closely bonded to their traditional cultural sources.

General Behavioral Characteristics

Literature across disciplines has identified certain types of behavior associated with certain cultural groups (Atkinson & Gim, 1989; Baca & Cervantes, 1989; Leung, 1988; Payne & Payne, 1989; Peterson & Ishii-Jordan, 1994). One example of a behavioral characteristic is externalized locus of control, which has been found more commonly among non-Caucasian-American cultural groups. This behavior assumes that the control over what happens in one's life is determined by forces out of one's hands (e.g., nature, God, spirits, the government). This type of thinking implies that individuals do not have the ability to change the way things are. They must accept that if their behaviors or circumstances do change, this will occur because of some intervention of external forces.

Another behavioral characteristic, often seen among Asian Americans, is an internalized means of managing reactions to environmental and intrapersonal stimuli. Those exhibiting this type of behavior do not express how they are feeling nor demonstrate negative emotions. The belief is that it is better to keep it all to oneself. This characteristic can be valued in one cultural setting as a demonstration of perseverance or attainment of higher spiritual planes. Yet another culture will negatively view this behavior as docile or unhealthy.

A third general behavioral characteristic, commonly noted among African Americans, is externalized or demonstrative behaviors. On the other end of the spectrum from internalized behaviors, individuals with this characteristic are more likely to verbalize or demonstrate their emotions and thoughts. The belief is that active verbal and nonverbal communication is a very natural form of expression, even though others from a different cultural environment might feel this is an inappropriate behavior.

Each of the examples of general behavioral characteristics just listed can be considered a valued trait or a disturbing one. Given that these characteristics are indeed evident across broad cultural groups, it can be assumed that the behavioral manifestations associated with these characteristics will also be evident in school settings where students representing those cultural groups exist. However, there is a danger in applying such broad characteristics to *all* members of a particular racial or ethnic group.

Intragroup Differences

The ethnographic categories used to identify people in North America arbitrarily combine cultural groups of individuals based on visible aspects of race, ethnicity, or language. However, it is extremely important to recognize that *individuals* comprise these ethnic and racial categories. Individual differences abound within larger cultural groups. Such differences involve (but are not limited to) socioeconomic status, acculturation levels, languages, religions, child-rearing practices, decision-making practices, and physical appearances. These intragroup differences influence the ways individuals behave and interpret behaviors.

Socioeconomics. Educational opportunities can contribute to the socioeconomic differences that separate individuals within cultural categories. African Americans with professional occupations and more advanced formal education will have different life experiences than African Americans in depressed rural or urban circumstances. Hispanic Americans in a migrant farming lifestyle will have different economic concerns than Hispanic Americans eyeing corporate career moves.

The ethnographic categories used to identify people in North America arbitrarily combine cultural groups of individuals based on visible aspects of race, ethnicity, or language. However, it is extremely important to recognize that individuals comprise these ethnic and racial categories. Individual differences abound within larger cultural groups.

When a great disparity exists between a cultural/ familial interpretation of a child's behavior and the school's interpretation of that behavior, there is also likely to be a disagreement on how that behavior is viewed and handled.

Acculturation. Levels of acquired acculturation will override the general behavioral characteristics attributed to individuals in distinct cultural groups. The effects of generational status are prominent. That is, the further an individual is from immigration (their generational status) or psychosocial bonding with a natal culture, the more likely she or he will experience the effects of other cultural influences that modify this individual's values, beliefs, and behaviors. Asian Americans who have been raised and acculturated into the mainstream of American lifestyles will have very different social needs and beliefs than Asian Americans newly immigrated. Native Americans who were raised within traditional tribal communities will view values and priorities differently than Native Americans raised without strong cultural identification bonds.

Language. Although certain cultural similarities, such as a shared language, may imply a shared set of life experiences, differences do exist among ethnic groups speaking the same or relatively similar languages (Figueroa & Gallegos, 1978; Nuttall, Landurand, & Goldman, 1984). For example, German or Russian immigrants from Cold War European political situations will have more difficulty understanding U.S. society's social and educational expectations than immigrants from the same areas whose families have either experienced post-Cold-War Europe or have been in America for a couple generations.

Viewing Behavioral Differences

When a great disparity exists between a cultural/familial interpretation of a child's behavior and the school's interpretation of that behavior, there is also likely to be a disagreement on how that behavior is viewed and handled. Some of the differing concerns include

1. Certain behavioral manifestations may not be deemed pathologic or deviant among all cultural groups.

2. The stigma of the EBD label can be a negative mark in the cultural beliefs prominent among subgroups.

3. Interventions used with students whose behaviors or

emotional reactions are considered inappropriate to school personnel (i.e., those who make placement decisions) may not be consistent with the way the student's cultural group may handle the behavior.

In light of these concerns, an examination of some of the critical issues facing professionals who work with students identified as EBD follows.

Critical Issues

The current policy issue of prime importance appears to concern the definition and terminology of the special education category "serious emotional disturbance" (SED).

So overarching is the impact of cultural issues that they affect the category definition, assessment process, placement decisions, advocacy efforts, and training of professionals who work with these students. While special education programs overall are currently in the process of being redesigned, an important focus in examining the category concerned with EBD should be the population of students identified as needing these services. The overrepresentation of African American males and underrepresentation of Asian American students is obvious in this category. This concern of racial/ethnic representation is one that permeates the major issues in the EBD field.

Category Issues

The current policy issue of prime importance appears to concern the definition and terminology of the special education category, *serious emotional disturbance* (SED). In the late 1980s, the National Special Education and Mental Health Coalition was jointly founded by The Council for Exceptional Children and the National Mental Health Association. The purpose of this coalition was to discuss and formulate "policy goals and action statements" (Forness, 1988, p. 132) to address a variety of problems that exist for students with EBD. Although issues such as identification and assessment, delivery of appropriate services, and interagency coordination were generally agreed upon among the coalition members, consensus on the terminology and definition of this category of special education was more difficult to obtain. Of concern were

Without a clear definition of what constitutes education in the term "educational performance," inequitable treatment in accessing services will likely increase among students whose behaviors or conditions do not enable them to relate appropriately to peers and others in schools.

two phrases that tend to have a negative cultural impact: educational performance and social maladjustment.

Educational performance. Part of the reason for the coalition's diverse views was the difference in implied meaning of the present clause *adversely affects educational performance.* To see how this clause may contribute to the disparate treatment of CLD students who are evaluated for EBD, it is necessary to define the parameters of educational performance. Cline (1990) suggests that "ambiguity in language" (p. 160) is a policy problem that results in wide-ranging interpretation of eligibility. When so much liberty is given in interpreting the types of behaviors that make a child eligible for services, opportunities for discrimination can occur for select groups of students.

Without a clear definition of what constitutes education in the term *educational performance,* inequitable treatment in accessing services will likely increase among students whose behaviors or conditions do not enable them to relate appropriately to peers and others in schools. In asking the question "What is education?" the answers may focus on classrooms, curricular content, or cognitive development. Cline (1990) offers "a more defensible definition of education when it comes to deciding the eligibility of SED/BD students. 'Education is the ability to integrate into the school and community and be available for instruction'" (p. 165).

Social maladjustment. The eligibility for services of students with a *social maladjustment* problem raises additional concern in policy practices because there is no clear definition of the term. Furthermore, the practice of excluding from eligibility all students upon whose backs this term is placed was not the original intent of the Congress who passed the Education for All Handicapped Children legislation (Public Law 94-142). "Certainly, a general authorization to exclude students who are troublesome to school officials and expensive to serve can neither be inferred nor found anywhere in legislative history" (Cline, 1990, p. 170). America's inner cities and burgeoning penal institutions can testify to the fact that a disproportionate number of African American males occupies these habitats. When the term, social maladjustment, is given to these individuals based on behavioral manifestations, it removes the opportunity for these persons to receive special education services. Furthermore, it gives the appearance of a very discriminating action toward one cultural group.

Proposed terminology. A proposal for a new terminology for and definition of EBD was finally developed by the National Special Education and Mental Health Coalition. Besides the terminology and definition, the proposal defined the concept of educational performance. The term *emotional or behavioral disorder* was suggested to replace the federal term *seriously emotionally disturbed,* and the definition described inappropriate behaviors as "responses in school so different from appropriate age, cultural, or ethnic norms that they adversely affect educational performance. Educational performance includes the development and demonstration of academic, social, vocational, and personal skills" (Forness & Knitzer, 1991). Although controversy continues over the coalition's terminology and definition (McIntyre, 1993), the proposal is at least one suggestion for attempting to address the discriminating effect that the category of EBD has had on CLD students.

Assessment Issues

The eligibility criteria under P. L. 94-142 for determining whether a student is emotionally/behaviorally disordered in special education (based on conditions of duration, intensity and frequency) are listed as follows: (a) an inability to learn which cannot be explained by intellectual, sensory, or health factors; (b) an inability to build or maintain satisfactory interpersonal relationships with peers and teachers; (c) inappropriate types of behavior or feelings under normal circumstances; (d) a general pervasive mood of unhappiness or depression; or (e) a tendency to develop physical symptoms or fears associated with personal or school problems. It is a multidisciplinary team's responsibility to decide which of these characteristics the child exhibits.

Culturally influenced behaviors. The assessment process in special education enables a multidisciplinary team of professionals to evaluate a student, analyze the results of the evaluation, and make decisions on eligibility for special services. Because behavioral and emotional expressions are so powerfully tied to cultural experiences, interpreting behaviors exhibited by students requires that the professionals know the underlying experiences that have shaped

Because behavioral and emotional expressions are so powerfully tied to cultural experiences, interpreting behaviors exhibited by students requires that the professionals know the underlying experiences that have shaped the students' reactions to social situations.

the students' reactions to social situations. It is well known that the racial/ethnic backgrounds of students can lead teachers to perceive their behaviors differently (Carlson & Stephens, 1986; Emihovich, 1983).

Individual personalities and cultural environments influence the way people behave in certain circumstances. For example, unpredictable behaviors may be due to inconsistency of behaviors in the home (Horton & Hunt, 1968) or the mismatch between one culture's stimuli and another culture's interpretation of and response to the stimuli. Not demonstrating a visible response when defensive, angry, embarrassed, confused, or frustrated may be the general tendency of a cultural group. The conclusion of the school decision makers may be that the child is withdrawn or has some emotional difficulties.

In another example, physical display of power or strength may be a manifestation of an expected machismo attitude, the testing of physical ability, or the expected male dominant role (Foster, 1986; Hanna, 1988). Students who exhibit such behaviors may be doing what is culturally expected of them in developing toward adulthood. However, the school professionals may determine that such behavior is disrespectful or inappropriate.

In the last example, challenging the authority of school officials may satisfy the need to gain power for those in cultural groups who feel oppressed or believe they live in a powerless environment. Demonstrating this type of behavior may be the learned response to a feeling of helplessness that is perceived to be discriminatory.

The examples of behaviors just listed may be (a) acceptable in certain cultures, (b) part of the normal process one experiences when acculturating to a new group, or (c) necessary for survival in the student's cultural or physical environment. Recognizing the function or communicative intent of the behavior will be necessary to understand whether the behavior is disordered or not.

Acculturational behaviors. The acculturation process to mainstream American society can lead to behaviors that may be interpreted as pathological because stresses increase as one moves from one cultural set of norms to another (Gim, Atkinson, & Whiteley, 1990;

Ishii-Jordan & Peterson, 1994; Nuttall et al., 1984). For example, when a child moves from a patriarchal society where family members each have clearly defined roles (and the child's role is to be quiet and observing) to an environment where the child is expected to assume another family member's traditional role (e.g., interpreter, decision maker, assertive participant), the child can become confused and filled with stress. The expectations in the home and in his or her natal culture seem to clash with the expectations of the new environment. Negative types of behaviors may result as the child attempts to cope with the different expectations.

Care should be taken to ensure that the behaviors typically associated with acculturation and/or language acquisition are not mistakenly interpreted as long-term emotional or behavioral conditions. At the same time, school professionals should attempt to assist the child with understanding what is happening. Students with cultural and/or linguistic differences may (a) temporarily exhibit signs of behavior disorders because of recent traumatic experiences they have undergone as refugees or immigrants, (b) display behaviors deemed appropriate in their own cultural groups but unacceptable in the majority culture's expectations, (c) be inappropriately evaluated with assessment instruments discriminatory toward them, or (d) not receive necessary services because their behaviors are dismissed as solely a cultural difference rather than a genuine disorder (Morrow, 1994; Nuttall et al., 1984).

Language disorders and behavior. Behavior and language are intimately woven together because the behaviors an individual exhibits communicate her or his intentions, beliefs, or thoughts. In her literature search on assessing for language disorders among students with limited English proficiency (LEP), Langdon (1989) compiled a list of factors important to consider because they may *simulate* a language disorder:

1. Length of residence in U. S. (limited language exposure may give the appearance of a language disorder).

2. Attendance disruption of schooling (students have a decreased ability to acquire cognitive academic lan-

> *Care should be taken to ensure that the behaviors typically associated with acculturation and/or language acquisition are not mistakenly interpreted as long-term emotional or behavioral conditions.*

> *Behavior and language are intimately woven together because the behaviors an individual exhibits communicate her or his intentions, beliefs, or thoughts.*

Studies have shown that deficits in language skills are evident in students who have behavioral or emotional problems

guage proficiency [CALP] if they are not in school often).

3. Types of classrooms attended (differing methodologies used or differing language expectations can influence perceptions of a disorder).

4. Uses of language (the relevance or typical nature of a language task made not be deemed necessary, e.g., why should I retell an incident to someone who has already witnessed it?).

5. Peer comparisons (similar comparisons should be made, e.g., age groups, ethnic peers, family members).

6. Health and developmental factors.

Although her search revealed difficulty in formulating the definition of a language disorder in LEP students, it was clear that "if a language disorder is manifested in the primary language, it will also be reflected in the second language." (Langdon, 1989, p. 160).

Of course, language use in native English speakers also influences social and behavioral actions. Studies have shown that deficits in language skills are evident in students who have behavioral or emotional problems (Giddan, 1991; Rosenthal & Simeonsson, 1991; Ruhl, Hughes, & Camarata, 1992). Expressive and pragmatic language abilities help children maneuver with socially appropriate behaviors and allow them to select more socially appropriate problem-solving options. Students who have deficits in pragmatic language often engage in behaviors that put them at odds with their peers and adults, leading them toward the types and frequencies of inappropriate behaviors that serve as eligibility criteria for EBD services.

Collier (1987) found that older non-native-English-speaking children (ages 12 to 15) have the greatest difficulty with English acquisition for cognitive language purposes. It takes a longer period of time for them to acquire the complex language skills needed in the upper grades while they are mastering English. Pragmatic skills in language indicate a higher, more complex level of language proficiency. If children who are older in age when they arrive in this country require a greater amount of time reaching the more complex language activities, it might follow that pragmatic language proficiency may be deficient in such children. All this research in language and social behavior may have implications for interpreting and intervening with students who demonstrate poor behavioral choices regardless of their linguistic or dialectical background. The greater impact, however, may be on those students who are acquiring English as a new language.

Assessment practices. As long as assessment procedures include standardized assessment instruments, CLD students will be differentially impacted in special education classification systems (Reilly, 1991; Sugai, 1988). The eligibility criteria for EBD services is based on a subjective interpretation by evaluation teams, thereby creating great disparity in how one views the students referred for this special education category (Kauffman, 1985). The multidisciplinary teams that evaluate and make eligibility decisions in EBD do not always include persons who are aware of culturally influenced behavioral differences and the varying biased reactions that student behaviors can elicit from educators and professionals unfamiliar with cultural interpretations of students' behaviors.

The use of alternative authentic assessment practices in evaluating CLD students for special education services is important in eliminating extraneous, culturally based misperceptions. The difference between alternative and traditional assessment procedures is based on the method of accessing or gathering the data. Data gathering for assessment can be viewed in two groups: (a) standardized or traditional tests and (b) any other methods of acquiring information on the ability and growth of a student (Hughes, 1993). Collecting information through observations of students, interviews with the student and family members, and valuable input provided by cultural experts should be a standard procedure in assessment of students.

When a multidisciplinary team collects evaluative data on a CLD student's behavior, the cultural interpretations of those data must be included. If cultural considerations for the behavior are not examined, the values or beliefs of the team members may lead to an interpretation of the assessment data that is contrary to how the cultural group of the student might analyze it. Culturally or

Expressive and pragmatic language abilities help children maneuver with socially appropriate behaviors and allow them to select more socially appropriate problem-solving options.

*The use of
alternative
authentic
assessment
practices in
evaluating CLD
students for special
education services
is important in
eliminating
extraneous,
culturally based
misperceptions.*

linguistically diverse students are subject to inappropriate actions in the special education process from referral to identification (Council for Children with Behavioral Disorders, 1989). It is important that educators not fall into this discriminatory practice. Teachers and other professionals involved in prereferral and multidisciplinary evaluation teams must establish guidelines for collecting and evaluating behavioral data on CLD students that takes into account cultural influences.

Intervention Issues

Interventions used with students should vary depending on the cause for the behavioral manifestation. When educators and administrators are not prepared with an array of interventions, the most likely response to inappropriate behaviors of students is punishment. This is reflected in various school systems' codes of discipline whereby punishment, isolation, suspension, or exclusion may be more common consequences for negative behaviors than child conferencing or understanding culturally influenced behaviors.

*Without recognizing
and understanding
the underlying
motive that compels
the behavior, a
selected
intervention may
prove fruitless in
changing a
behavior.*

Underlying motives for behavior. Without recognizing and understanding the underlying motive that compels the behavior, a selected intervention may prove fruitless in changing a behavior. Special educators are taught to graph a baseline of a student's behaviors in order to determine the intensity, duration, or frequency of undesirable behaviors before proceeding with some type of behavioral intervention. The most common intervention model used in schools today is strongly behavioral in nature. While special education teachers maintain a number of interventions in their repertoire for handling behaviors they view as oppositional, reluctant, or inappropriate, the standard bag of tricks may not be effective as behavioral interventions if the underlying motive for the behavior is not determined. Approaching the student, the family, or cultural experts prior to selecting interventions may shed light on why certain behaviors are exhibited.

Types of interventions. The determination that a student with a particular racial/ethnic background has behavioral problems may influence the type of interventions teachers would likely use with these students (Ishii-Jordan, 1996). The interpretation of culturally based behaviors can also influence the type of strategies used to promote student cooperation in school (McIntyre, 1993). The teaching methods and techniques used in the classroom and the expectations teachers have for behaviors can have both positive and negative effects on CLD students. Teachers must recognize that students' learning styles, assumptions about formal education, comfort level in overt social relationships, and other culturally influenced factors impact how a student responds to the teacher's classroom style and behavioral expectations. The use of visual versus kinesthetic styles, competitive versus cooperative activities, private versus public demonstrations, and peer versus cross-age learning are all examples of ways to modify teaching techniques and behavioral interventions.

The inability to understand the effect that teachers' culturally based beliefs and interpretations (however naive) have on students' behavioral responses can only lead to continued misunderstandings and misinterpretations among teachers and students who do not share the same cultural backgrounds. Teachers must be open to examining different philosophical bases that may drive the selection of interventions to be used with students. They must be willing to expand their repertoire of interventions that will help students understand and modify behaviors considered inappropriate or unacceptable in particular educational settings.

Although the analysis of assessment data provides educators with the foundation for what and how to teach students, a search of the literature by Zigmond and Miller (1986) revealed that many teachers "plan and execute special education programs on the basis of subjective impressions" or "intuitive judgments" relative to students (p. 507). Interventions are selected based on gut feelings. For a culturally competent and experienced teacher who uses nonbiased evaluations and approaches based on genuine student needs, this personal judgment may prove highly beneficial for individualizing education. However, the danger also exists for teachers without cultural understanding (gained from personal experience and/or acquired knowledge) and without a teaching philosophy that emphasizes equity for all students to discriminate in both assessment data gathering and intervention choices with CLD students.

Approaching the student, the family, or cultural experts prior to selecting interventions may shed light on why certain behaviors are exhibited.

Part of the culturally sensitive education must include recognition of the communication differences that exist and the adjustments needed when assessing CLD students

Training and Development Issues

Changes in policy, assessment practices, and interventions can only occur when the professionals who work with CLD students having emotional or behavioral problems recognize the paradigms and practices they use with these students. As new information is gleaned through research and experience with a changing population of students in today's schools, continual updating of education professionals' own cognitive and experiential learning must occur.

Cultural competence. The initial training and subsequent professional development of teachers and other educational personnel must be examined to include culturally competent knowledge and practice. Institutions of higher education must provide alternative and culturally sensitive training programs for psychologists and other professionals who evaluate students for EBD program placement. Part of the culturally sensitive education must include recognition of the communication differences that exist and the adjustments needed when assessing CLD students (Sue & Sue, 1990). The assessment issues covered earlier in this chapter for this population of students must be addressed in training or development programs.

Although it may be difficult for individuals outside a particular cultural population to fully understand and serve the needs of students from that cultural group, it is not impossible to assist educational personnel in developing an understanding of differences and similarities among cultural groups and becoming competent in the notion that culturally based behaviors may vary among culturally different populations. It is also important that cultural competence training include the fact that many differences exist among individuals within cultural groups. Professional development, whether through preservice (college) or inservice means, can educate teachers and other professionals who work with CLD students.

Aspects of teacher development. Low tolerance for students with behavioral or emotional problems and lack of training in the use of appropriate interventions for problem students may very well produce the negative effects that EBD students have on teachers. The ability of teachers to provide an appropriate and effective educational experience for their students (with or without special needs) may be based on four aspects of teacher development:

1. The preparation teachers receive in understanding students relative to teaching and learning dimensions.

2. Teachers' knowledge of their subject matter.

3. The perceived sense of teaching efficacy teachers possess.

4. The perceived ability teachers have to generalize their skills to a real classroom setting. (Moeller & Ishii-Jordan, 1996)

These aspects of teacher development are useful for educators working with CLD students who have behavioral difficulties in the school setting. Gaining knowledge in cultural competence, in cross-cultural behavioral manifestations, in behavioral and instructional strategies, and in language/dialectical development would give teachers the necessary competence in the first area of teacher development just listed. Providing undergraduate and graduate students with the opportunity to study under persons with diverse cultural backgrounds and work with children in the school settings who have diverse behavioral and learning needs would give them the foundation for recognizing the many interpretations of behavior that exist and for acquiring a large repertoire of interventions to consider when working with CLD students.

Providing undergraduate and graduate students with the opportunity to study under persons with diverse cultural backgrounds and work with children in the school settings who have diverse behavioral and learning needs would give them the foundation for recognizing the many interpretations of behavior that exist and for acquiring a large repertoire of interventions to consider when working with CLD students.

Future Directions

Given the emerging literature base and current practices surrounding the restructuring of schools and of service delivery models in special education as well as the newly emerging demographic face of the student body, it is important to focus on philosophical models that produce *positive* school change. A more consistent definition of students who have behavioral concerns must be adopted across state and province boundaries so that interpretations of student behaviors are not prone to discriminatory biases. More research in authentic assessment-intervention processes should be

"Different cultures have different cognitive competencies and different rates of advancing through cognitive levels" (Roberts & DeBlassie, 1983, p. 841).

conducted with CLD students who have behavioral or emotional problems. Finally, a greater recruitment effort of both culturally diverse professionals and individuals with culturally competent training must occur if solutions are to be found for the problems in the EBD field that adversely affect CLD students.

Modifying Assessment and Intervention Practices

The issues addressed in this chapter that may most directly impact classroom teachers and other professionals in their work with CLD students with behavioral problems involve assessment and intervention practices. The whole challenge of assessment practices and procedures in identifying and planning strategies for CLD students with behavioral or emotional concerns must be comprehensively addressed and remedied in special education programs across the country. The traditional use of standardized assessments for CLD students has consistently demonstrated flaws in identification and placement for EBD programs. Roberts and DeBlassie (1983) emphasize that "different cultures have different cognitive competencies and different rates of advancing through cognitive levels" as well as "differing skills needed to cope with a particular culture" (p. 841). Traditional assessment practices must change.

Although a variety of informal or other assessment practices (e.g., performance assessment, portfolios, observation) are preferred over traditional assessments, not all can be considered authentic (Hughes, 1993). Given that authentic alternative assessment practices are becoming the preferred method of acquiring data on a student to determine both eligibility status for special education services and appropriate instructional behavioral methodologies in the classroom, the necessity to use alternative and authentic practices in assessing CLD students is even greater because of the discriminatory and incompatible cultural consequences associated with diverse learners and majority practices in educational settings.

A more dynamic process closely combining assessment and intervention would be more beneficial for students whose cultural backgrounds influence behaviors that may not be in an acceptable range of standards for the school environment. Perhaps schools might look beyond just a pure behavioral model of interventions to models that might consider more fully the diversity of cultural behaviors and philosophical notions supporting those behaviors.

Alternative Models

Functional behavioral analysis. Sugai (1988) proposed a model based in social learning theory that involves using a functional analysis to determine the functional relationships of the targeted behaviors to the antecedents and consequences of those behaviors. Interventions determined appropriate for students would be based on an "analysis of the communicative function of behavior" (Sugai, 1988, p. 73). Because one type of behavior may communicate very different intents among diverse cultures, the critical-effect concept that ties together the behavioral assessment and the intervention for a student may be much more nonbiased.

Circle of courage. Another example of an assessment and intervention process that may be associated more closely with a developmental or social learning school of thought is that proposed by Brendtro, Brokenleg, and Van Bockern (1990). It arises from Native American cultural traditions of examining how a child's misbehavior may be linked to a "broken" part of the child's circle of courage. In their model, a child's circle may be broken in any one of four areas: belonging, mastery, independence, or generosity. Assisting a student to heal or complete the circle through interventions involving communication, modeling, or providing successful opportunities for the child would be the adult's role in helping the child to change his or her behaviors and mend the circle.

Difference versus disorder. Disproportionate representation of CLD students in many areas of special education has been a continuing phenomenon for three decades. Artiles and Trent (1994) explicitly summarize that "the distinction between *to have* something that makes you different (e.g., a disabling condition) or *to be* different (e.g., to be culturally different) brings into the equation moral and ethical issues germane to the reform of identification, assessment, and intervention practices." (p. 426). Professionals must have the ability to recognize when behavior differences are not behavior disorders so that the overidentification of culturally diverse students with EBD will be eliminated.

Perhaps schools might look beyond just a pure behavioral model of interventions to models that might consider more fully the diversity of cultural behaviors and philosophical notions supporting those behaviors.

Professionals must have the ability to recognize when behavior differences are not behavior disorders so that the overidentification of culturally diverse students with EBD will be eliminated.

References

Artiles, A. J., & Trent, S. C. (1994). Overrepresentation of minority students in special education: A continuing debate. *The Journal of Special Education, 27,* 410-437.

Atkinson, R. A., & Gim, R. H. (1989). Asian-American cultural identity and attitudes toward mental health services. *Journal of Counseling Psychology, 36*(2), 209-212.

Baca, L. M., & Cervantes, H. T. (1989). *The bilingual special education interface* (2nd ed.). Columbus, OH: Merrill.

Brendtro, L., Brokenleg, M., & Van Bockern, S. (1990). *Reclaiming youth at risk: Our hope for the future.* Bloomington, IN: National Educational Service.

Carlson, P. E., & Stephens, T. M. (1986). Cultural bias and identification of behaviorally disordered children. *Behavioral Disorders, 11,* 191-199.

Cline, D. H. (1990). A legal analysis of policy initiatives to exclude handicapped/disruptive students from special education. *Behavioral Disorders, 15,* 159-173.

Collier, V. P. (1987). Age and rate of acquisition of second language for academic purposes. *TESOL Quarterly, 21,* 617-641.

Council for Children with Behavioral Disorders. (1989). Best assessment practices for students with behavioral disorders: Accommodation to cultural diversity and individual differences. *Behavioral Disorders, 14,* 263-278.

Emihovich, C. A. (1983). The color of misbehaving: Two case studies of deviant boys. *The Journal of Black Studies, 13,* 259-274.

Figueroa, R. A., & Gallegos, E. A. (1978). Ethnic differences in school behavior. *Sociology of Education, 51,* 289-298.

Forness, S. R. (1988). Planning for the needs of children with serious emotional disturbance: The national special education and mental health coalition. *Behavioral Disorders, 13,* 127-133.

Forness, S., & Knitzer, J. (1991). *A new proposed definition and terminology to replace 'serious emotional disturbance' in Individuals with Disabilities Education Act.* Alexandria, VA: National Mental Health and Special Education Coalition.

Foster, H. (1986). *Ribbin', jivin', and playin' the dozens.* New York: Ballantine.

Giddan, J. J. (1991). School children with emotional problems and communication deficits: Implications for speech-language pathologists. *Language, Speech, and Hearing Services in Schools, 22,* 291-295.

Gim, R. H., Atkinson, D. R., & Whiteley, S. (1990). Asian-American acculturation, severity of concerns, and willingness to see a counselor. *Journal of Counseling Psychology, 37,* 281-285.

Hanna, J. (1988). *Disruptive school behavior: Class, race, and culture.* New York: Homes & Meier.

Horton, P., & Hunt, C. (1968). *Sociology* (2nd ed.). New York: McGraw-Hill.

Hughes, S. (1993). What is alternative/authentic assessment and how does it impact special education? *Educational Horizons, 71*(1), 28-35.

Ishii-Jordan, S. R. (1996). *Interventions with diverse students having problem behaviors.* Manuscript submitted for publication.

Ishii-Jordan, S., & Peterson, R. L. (1994). Behavioral disorders in culture and community. In R. L. Peterson & S. Ishii-Jordan (Eds.), *Multicultural issues in the education of students with behavioral disorders* (pp. 251-262). Cambridge, MA: Brookline.

Johnson, A. (1987). Attitudes toward mainstreaming: Implications for inservice training and teaching the handicapped. *Education, 107,* 229-233.

Kauffman, J. (1985). *Characteristics of children's behavior disorders* (3rd ed.). Columbus, OH: Merrill.

Langdon, H. W. (1989). Language disorder or difference? Assessing the language skills of Hispanic students. *Exceptional Children, 56,* 160-167.

Leung, E. K. (1988). Cultural and acculturational commonalities and diversities among Asian Americans: Identification and programming considerations. In A. A. Ortiz & B. A. Ramirez (Eds.). *Schools and the culturally diverse exceptional student: Promising practices and future directions* (pp. 86-95). Reston, VA: The Council for Exceptional Children.

McIntyre, T. (1993). Reflections on the new definition for emotional or behavioral disorders: Who still falls through the cracks and why. *Behavioral Disorders, 18,* 148-160.

Moeller, A. J., & Ishii-Jordan, S. (1996). Teacher efficacy: A model for teacher development and inclusion. *Journal of Behavioral Education, 6,* 293-310.

Morrow, R. D. (1994). Immigration, refugee, and generational status as related to behavioral disorders. In R. L. Peterson & S. Ishii-Jordan (Eds.), *Multicultural issues in the education of students with behavioral disorders* (pp. 196-207). Cambridge, MA: Brookline.

Nuttall, E. V., Landurand, P. M., & Goldman, P. (1984). A critical look at testing and evaluation from a cross-cultural perspective. In P. C. Chinn (Ed.), *Education of culturally and linguistically different exceptional children* (pp. 42-62). Reston, VA: The Council for Exceptional Children.

Payne, B. D., & Payne, D. A. (1989). Sex, race, and grade differences in the locus of control orientations of at-risk elementary students. *Psychology in the Schools, 26,* 84-88.

Peterson, R. L., & Ishii-Jordan, S. (1994). *Multicultural issues in the education of students with behavioral disorders.* Cambridge, MA: Brookline.

Reilly, T. F. (1991). Cultural bias: The albatross of assessing behavior-disordered children and youth. *Preventing School Failure, 36*(1), 50-53.

Roberts, E., & DeBlassie, R. R. (1983). Test bias and the culturally different early adolescent. *Adolescence, 18,* 837-843.

Rosenthal, S. L., & Simeonsson, R. J. (1991). Communication skills in emotionally disturbed and nondisturbed adolescents. *Behavioral Disorders, 16,* 192-199.

Ruhl, K. L., Hughes, C. A., & Camarata, S. M. (1992). Analysis of the expressive and receptive language characteristics of emotionally handicapped students served in public school settings. *Journal of Childhood Communication Disorders, 14,* 165-176.

Sue, D. W., & Sue, D. (1990). *Counseling the culturally different: Theory and practice* (2nd ed.). New York: Wiley.

Sugai, G. (1988). Educational assessment of the culturally diverse and behavior disordered student: An examination of critical effect. In A. A. Ortiz & B. A. Ramirez (Eds.), *Schools and the culturally diverse exceptional student: Promising practices and future directions* (pp. 63-75). Reston, VA: The Council for Exceptional Children.

Zigmond, N., & Miller, S. E. (1986). Assessment for instructional planning. *Exceptional Children, 52,* 501-509.

4 From Tests to Talking in the Classroom: Assessing Communicative Competence

Grace Zamora-Durán
The Council for Exceptional Children

Elba I. Reyes
University of Arizona

Across the nation, educators face the challenge of teaching students whose first language is other than English. These are not teachers of English as a Second Language (ESL) but content area teachers in regular classrooms (Reyes & Bos, in press). Very often these students may demonstrate limited language skills in their primary language (Carrasquillo, 1990) that may slow down second language learning as well as affect their communication competency, that is, the ability to communicate effectively. These factors may preclude academic success (Reyes, 1994), lead to special education referrals and eventually placement, and contribute to the disproportionate representation of linguistically and culturally diverse (CLD) students in special education programs.

Educators can begin to address the disproportionate representation of LEP students by appropriately assessing and determining the true language proficiencies of bilingual children.

Disproportionate representation of limited-English-proficient (LEP) students has been documented since the early 1980s (Maheady, Towne, Algozzine, Mercer, & Ysseldyke, 1983; Ortiz & Yates, 1983; Wright & Santa Cruz, 1983) and will continue to be an issue with the growing numbers of students in today's classrooms who are classified as ESL learners (National Center for Education Statistics, 1994). Educators can begin to address the disproportionate representation of LEP students by appropriately assessing and determining the true language proficiencies of bilingual children.

A practical alternative to traditional language-proficiency tests is determining students' proficiency in natural contexts.

To make appropriate instructional decisions, practitioners need viable indicators of students' level of language skills. This chapter presents information that education professionals can use to identify students' existing language skills and determine their language needs.

Beyond Traditional Language-Proficiency Measures

Unfortunately, many language-proficiency tests currently in use do not give teachers the information needed to develop appropriate lessons or to identify teaching strategies that could help ESL students improve their English skills. The tests, which attempt to simulate natural language situations, measure isolated skills and provide composite scores that yield little insight into a student's true level of language abilities. For teachers to help their ESL students, they must be able to enhance the information gleaned from such tests with other sources of information. One such source is classroom observations.

A practical alternative to traditional language-proficiency tests is determining students' proficiency in natural contexts. This way the teacher obtains a more accurate picture of the student's actual functioning level (Fradd, 1996; Wells, 1986; Wong-Fillmore, 1983). The classroom is one such context. Periodic classroom observations can yield valuable data on students' language skills, areas of need, and progress (Zamora-Durán, 1991). Teachers can then create learning environments that give students opportunities to practice the skills they need to be proficient in English. An excellent method to use for observing students' language abilities is to observe their levels of communicative competency.

Communicative Competence

Communicative competence describes language proficiency as real or authentic conversational factors, including the ability to comprehend language. Assessing language from a communicative competence perspective provides the opportunity to assess language in natural settings. A communicative competence approach looks at the students' knowledge in using appropriate language in specific or different contexts, including the knowledge of when to speak and be silent, when to use formal or informal register, and how to adjust language to accommodate the needs of different listeners (Canale, 1981). To assess students' communicative competence, education professionals look at four areas or categories of language skills: (a) grammatical competence, (b) sociolinguistic competence, (c) discourse competence, and (d) strategic competence (Canale, 1981; Canale & Swain, 1980; Kayser, 1993). Figure 4.1 provides a checklist of these four categories and the corresponding language skills.

Grammatical Competence

A student demonstrates grammatical competence when he or she achieves mastery of lexical items, rules of word and sentence formation, literal meaning, pronunciation, and spelling. When a student is acquiring a second language, grammatical skills are the most difficult, and sometimes the last, to be mastered.

The following illustrates the type of data provided by a typical language assessment instrument and information that can be captured from observing students' language use in the classroom:

> *Information from a language assessment test:* Jose, age 12 , scored "limited," on the English section and "proficient" on the Spanish portion of the proficiency test.

> *Information from a communication competence checklist:* The grammatical portion of Figure 4.1 would reflect the skills that the student demonstrated, and the teacher would add to this information with observation notes (see, for example, Figure 4.2).

Sociolinguistic Competence

Students demonstrate sociolinguistic competence when they use language appropriately in different social contexts, with emphasis on meanings and forms. For example, students who use terms of endearment or express themselves courteously by using titles of respect and terms of etiquette can be described as "sociolinguistically" competent. Also, students who use an informal dialect with

A communicative competence approach looks at the students' knowledge in using appropriate language in specific or different contexts, including the knowledge of when to speak and be silent, when to use formal or informal register, and how to adjust language to accommodate the needs of different listeners.

It must be remembered that communication is not merely form and structure: To communicate, individuals must understand each others' intent.

friends and a more formal dialect with adults demonstrate their sociolinguistic competence. Students who have not yet mastered sociolinguistic competency may at times appear to be disrespectful.

A sample sociolinguistic column (see Figure 4.3) indicates Eduardo's use of the title of respect along with his use of the informal register when speaking to his peers. The teacher's observation notes again enhance the information on the chart.

Discourse Competence

The essence of communication is encapsuled within discourse competence. When a student achieves discourse competence, language is used in an organized and effective manner. The student uses pronouns and transition words appropriately and uses repetition to make a point. Discourse competence also includes discussing a topic with consistency and presenting ideas relevant to the ongoing discussion.

Students can contribute to conversations with information that is important and germane to the discussion at hand while their syntax or pronunciation may not demonstrate grammatical competence. It must be remembered that communication is not merely form and structure: To communicate, individuals must understand each others' intent. In Figure 4.4, which provides a sample of the student's skill level within the discourse competence category, the teacher observed that Sonia understood the language task but was unable to communicate her intent. The lack of check marks in the column is an indication of the student's needs in this area. Again, the teacher's observation notes help to identify which skills to focus on when developing an instructional program.

Strategic Competence

A student demonstrates strategic competence when verbal and nonverbal strategies (such as paraphrasing and gesturing) are used to enhance the effectiveness of the communication and to compensate for breakdowns in communication due to performance limitations.

An example of strategic competence is code switching, or alternating between two languages. Code switching has been de-

Figure 4.1

Checklist for Skills Illustrating Communicative Competency

✔	Grammatical	✔	Sociolinguistic	✔	Discourse	✔	Strategic
	Uses noun/verb agreement		Demonstrates various styles of social register in speech, for example, when interacting with peers or adults		Retells an event with attention to sequence		Joins groups and acts as if understands language and activities
	Uses pronouns correctly		Uses diminutives		Explains activity in present or near future		Demonstrates expressive ability
	Uses proper syntax		Uses terms of endearment		Shares experiences spontaneously		Counts on friends for help
	Uses verb tenses appropriately		Uses courtesy, etiquette terms, and titles of respect		Tells stories with personal emphases		Switches language to resolve ambiguities
	Uses dialectical variations		Uses appropriate variations in intonation		Switches language for elaboration		Observes and imitates language patterns
	Uses complex sentence structure				Switches language to clarify statements		Asks for information
					Switches language to experiment with new language		Reads to gain information
							Uses a dictionary
							Asks for repetition
							Takes risks and guesses at language meaning
							Attempts difficult words and constructions

Code switching is not detrimental to learning. Rather, it encourages students to respond in either language and provides them with an expressive facility to demonstrate their actual level of comprehension.

Figure 4.2

Sample Grammatical Section of the Skills Checklist

✔	Grammatical
	Uses noun/verb agreement
	Uses pronouns correctly
✔	Uses proper syntax
✔	Uses verb tenses appropriately
	Uses dialectical variations
✔	Uses complex sentence structure

Teacher Observation Notes: Jose's response to one of my questions during social studies: "It said that the state was named Franklin and that lasted for four years." His use of English indicates that he can respond in complete sentences, that he is understanding word order in English. He appears to be developing a functional use of English.

scribed as a skill and a resource for negotiating participation and mediating comprehension. Code switching is not detrimental to learning. Rather, it encourages students to respond in either language and provides them with an expressive facility to demonstrate their actual level of comprehension (Reyes, Zamora-Durán, & Bos, 1989).

Figure 4.3

Sample Sociolinguistic Section of the Skills Checklist

✔	**Sociolinguistic**
✔	Demonstrates various styles of social register in speech, for example, when interacting with peers or adults
	Uses diminutives
	Uses terms of endearment
✔	Uses courtesy, etiquette terms, and titles of respect
	Uses appropriate variations in intonation

Teacher Observation Notes: Eduardo, speaking to a small group of girls during their small group work: "She say we can look at the map. Let me see your map!" He then said to me: "Miss, right we not cheating if we look at the map?"

Teachers who do not speak the student's first language need to contextualize the information being presented.

In the sample illustrated in Figure 4.5, the teacher encourages the student to communicate his idea with his peers. Teachers who do not speak the student's first language need to contextualize the information being presented. This can be accomplished by showing pictures and providing the appropriate vocabulary, by using videos or CD-ROMs, or by having students work together in small groups. Then the teacher can observe whether the student is integrating the modeled language skills.

Figure 4.4

**Sample Discourse Section
of the Skills Checklist**

✔	Discourse
	Retells an event with attention to sequence
	Explains activity in present or near future
	Shares experiences spontaneously
	Tells stories with personal emphases
	Switches language for elaboration
	Switches language to clarify statements
	Switches language to experiment with new language

Teacher Observation Notes: Sonia's weakest area appears to be discourse competence. She has difficulty speaking cohesively: her utterances are short and fragmented which make her ideas appear to be unrelated. Today we talked about jobs that provide services. When asked what her mom did, Sonia responded, "Beds." However, after further probing I learned that her mom works for Housekeeping in a local hotel. Sonia does not stray from the topic being discussed but is still having difficulty making herself understood.

Figure 4.5
Sample Strategic Section
of the Skills Checklist

✔	Strategic
✔	Joins groups and acts as if understands language and activities
	Demonstrates expressive ability
✔	Counts on friends for help
✔	Switches language to resolve ambiguities
✔	Observes and imitates language patterns
	Asks for information
	Reads to gain information
	Uses a dictionary
	Asks for repetition
	Takes risks and guesses at language meaning
	Attempts difficult words and constructions

Teacher Observation Notes: Today, Jose was trying to elaborate a concept we were discussing. He appropriately code switched when he lacked a word in English and asked one of his peers to translate for me. I provided the word in English which he then repeated. However, I noticed that at times he seemed to lack the word in both languages.

Classroom observations rely heavily on teachers' input, which is directly influenced by their beliefs and perceptions. Therefore, teachers need to be aware of their beliefs about, perceptions of, and expectations for students being observed. In this way, they can ensure that their observations and comments remain objective and constructive.

Clearly the information teachers obtained by viewing their students' language and by applying the communicative competence approach is more useful than a score of 2 (limited) in English and 5 (proficient) in Spanish. Remember, language acquisition is a process, and skills will be mastered over time when opportunities are provided to develop and practice those skills. With the tool in Figure 4.1, teachers can tell what progress the student is making in English development and plan instructional activities that build on those skills the student already possesses.

Conclusion

Although educators agree on the importance of determining the language proficiency of limited-English-speaking students, how to determine proficiency is still being debated. This chapter illustrates the feasibility of determining students' language proficiency through classroom observations, supports the idea of assessing language in natural contexts, and presents the viability of the concept of communicative competence to gauge students' language development and progress. In addition, samples have been provided that illustrate how communicative competence presents a more global and comprehensive understanding of students' language than do traditional language-proficiency measures.

Classroom observations rely heavily on teachers' input, which is directly influenced by their beliefs and perceptions. Therefore, teachers need to be aware of their beliefs about, perceptions of, and expectations for students being observed. In this way, they can ensure that their observations and comments remain objective and constructive.

When using categories of communicative competence, teachers have access to richer and more meaningful information to analyze their students' language. Using the checklist, teachers can verify emerging language and identify which skills still need to be developed. They can plan meaningful activities to address their students' language needs by building on the students' language resources and by pooling the students' language resources and abilities to address the language needs of the class.

Author Note

Research presented in this chapter was funded as part of a grant (H023B00025) from the Office of Special Education and Rehabilitative Services, U. S. Department of Education.

References

Canale, M. (1981). From communicative competence to communicative language pedagogy. In J. Richard & R. Schmidt (Eds.), *Language and communication* (pp. 1-27). New York: Longman.

Canale, M. & Swain, M. (1980). Theoretical bases of communicative approaches to second language teaching and testing. *Applied Linguistics, 1,* 1-47.

Carrasquillo, A. L. (1990). Instructional language preferences of bilingual elementary learning disabled students. In A. L. Carrasquillo & R. E. Baecher (Eds.), *Teaching the bilingual special education student* (pp. 90-106). Norwood, NJ: Ablex Publishing.

Fradd, S. (1996, April). *El-SOL (Exceptional learners-speakers of other languages): Providing appropriate services to LEP exceptional students.* Paper presented at the Annual Convention of The Council for Exceptional Children, Orlando, FL.

Kayser, H. (1993). Hispanic cultures. In D.E. Battle (Ed.), *Communication disorders in multicultural populations* (pp. 114 - 152). Boston: Andover Medical Publishers.

Maheady, L., Towne, R., Algozzine, B., Mercer, J., & Ysseldyke, J. (1983). Minority overrepresentation: A case for alternative practices prior to referral. *Learning Disability Quarterly, 6*(4), 448-456.

National Center for Education Statistics. (1994). *The pocket condition of education.* Washington, DC: U.S. Department of Education, Office of Educational Research and Improvement.

Ortiz, A. A., & Yates, J. (1983). Incidence of exceptionality among Hispanics: Implications for manpower planning. *Journal of National Association for Bilingual Education, 7*(2), 41-53.

Reyes, E. I. (1990). The thinking, reading, writing connection: Facilitating the process with learning activities. *Cognition and Instruction, 7*(2), 117-175.

Reyes, E. I. (1994). *Classroom discourse communicative competency of bilingual students with learning disabilities during content learning in three learning environments.* Unpublished doctoral dissertation, University of Arizona, Tucson.

Reyes, E. I., & Bos, C. S. (in press). Interactive semantic mapping and charting: Enhancing content area learning for language minority students. In R. Gersten & R. T. Jimenez (Eds.), *Promoting learning for culturally and linguistically diverse students: Classroom application from contemporary research.* Pacific Grove, CA: Brooks/Cole Publishing.

Reyes, E. I., Zamora-Durán, G., & Bos, C. S. (1989). Language as a resource for mediating comprehension. In S. McCormick & J. Zutell (Eds.), *Thirty-eighth yearbook of the National Reading Conference: Cognitive and social perspectives for literacy research and instruction* (pp. 253-260). Chicago: National Reading Conference.

Wells, G. (1986). *The meaning makers: Children learning language and using language to learn.* Portsmouth, NH: Heinemann.

Wong-Fillmore, L. (1983). The language learner as an individual: Implications of research on individual differences for the ESL teacher. In M. A. Clarue & J. Handscombe (Eds.), *On TESOL 1982: Pacific perspectives on language learning and teaching* (pp. 157-171). Washington, DC: Teaching English as a Second or Other Language.

Wright, P., & Santa Cruz, R. (1983). Ethnic composition of special education programs in California. *Learning Disability Quarterly, 6*(4), 387-394.

Zamora-Durán, G. (1991) *Language proficiency, reading achievement, language of instruction of Hispanic limited-English-proficient elementary school-aged students.* Unpublished doctoral dissertation, University of Arizona, Tucson.

5 Disproportionate Representation in Gifted Programs: Best Practices for Meeting This Challenge

James M. Patton
The College of William and Mary

Identifying and nurturing the talent of learners in public schools has historically been a challenge to psychometricians, psychologists, and educators. A larger challenge has been the task of assessing, identifying, and nurturing the talents and gifts of culturally and linguistically diverse (CLD) learners. Recent data indicate that CLD individuals are generally disproportionately represented in 30% to 70% of gifted programs in American public schools (Richert, 1987) and represent a large untapped reservoir of talent (Zappia, 1989). Zappia reported that in 1987

- Caucasian Americans represented 71.2% of the public school population and 81.4% of the gifted program population.

- African-Americans represented 16.2% of the public school population and 8.4% of the gifted program population.

- Hispanics represented 9.1% of the public school population and 4.7% of the gifted program population.

- Asians represented 2.5% of the public school population and 5.0% of the gifted program population.

While a number of causative factors for the disproportionate representation of CLD learners in gifted programs has been offered, only slight progress correcting the imbalances has been made.

Contemporary schools and society continue to be challenged to assess, identify, unearth, and nurture the talents and gifts of large numbers of African Americans, Hispanics, Native Americans, and certain Asian American populations. The way that the educational system responds to this challenge could determine the future of American society.

Contemporary schools and society continue to be challenged to assess, identify, unearth, and nurture the talents and gifts of large numbers of African Americans, Hispanics, Native Americans, and certain Asian American populations. The way that the educational system responds to this challenge could determine the future of American society.

Unlike this book's other chapters, which focus on techniques for reducing the disproportionate representation of CLD students in certain special education programs, this chapter highlights ideas, strategies, and techniques practitioners can use to *increase the number of CLD learners identified for gifted programs.* The purposes, then, of this chapter are to discuss current concepts of intelligence and giftedness, identify general ideas and strategies that practitioners can use to more effectively nurture the talent development of CLD learners, and offer culturally specific strategies that increase the number of CLD students identified for and served in gifted programs. To place these issues in their proper sociocultural and political context, a brief discussion of major definitions of intelligence and giftedness and ways of identifying these constructs is offered.

Definitions of Intelligence and Giftedness

Recently, the Board of Scientific Affairs of the American Psychological Association commissioned Ulric Neisser and colleagues to conduct a review of the "approaches to intelligence that are currently influential, or that seem to be becoming so" (Neisser et al., 1996, p. 77). These researchers reported that most constructs of intelligence have taken a psychometric approach growing out of the Western European tradition of defining intelligence as a discrete, unitary construct that could be measured by a paper-and-pencil test. As Neisser et al. (1996) point out, some of these intelligence tests proclaim to measure a particular variable, such as verbal intelligence or inductive reasoning, while other, more familiar individual measures, such as the Stanford-Binet and Wechsler tests, purport to measure both verbal and nonverbal items.

Traditionally, high performance on group or individual intelligence tests is often used as the single criterion and major pathway in the process of screening and identifying students for gifted and talented programs. The pervasive and compulsive inclination to use these tests can be seen in the fact that many states while not requiring a particular IQ cutoff score still use these tests because of the mythology around their ease of use and their so-called objectivity and ability to predict intelligence and giftedness. With the exception, however, of certain Asian Americans (those of Chinese and Japanese extraction), CLD students overall score lower on these tests. The mean IQ scores of Hispanic Americans (to include Puerto Ricans, Mexican Americans, Central and South Americans, and Cubans), African Americans, and members of culturally distinct North American Indian tribes are lower than the mean IQ score of Caucasian Americans, thereby mitigating against their inclusion in gifted and talented programs (Neisser et al., 1996). These tests enjoy widespread use even though attacks on the unfairness of the tests themselves as well as on the cultural incongruence among the test developers, test givers, and test takers are legion (Dixon, 1976; Gould, 1981; Patton, 1993, 1996; Weinberg, 1989).

Neisser et al. (1996) offered another critique of intelligence tests by providing research indicating that IQ alone fails to capture the full range of an individual's intelligence, cognition, ability, or talent. More recently, spurred by changes in the larger sociocultural and political body politic and advances in human science theory, researchers and academics, such as Gardner (1983) and Sternberg (1985), have advanced constructs of intelligence and giftedness that are multidimensional. Sternberg's triarchic theory of intelligence and Gardner's seven-intelligences theory of multiple intelligences have attracted considerable interest among human science theorists and practitioners. Their work represents examples of pluralistic views of intelligence and giftedness that recognize the many manifestations of giftedness within the context of one's own culture. Sternberg's (1991) analytic, synthetic, and practical intelligences and Gardner's linguistic, musical, logical-mathematical, spatial, body-kinesthetic, and intra- and interpersonal intelligences serve as models for the further development of a multimodal model of intelligence and giftedness. Both of these groundbreaking theories represent a move from exclusion to inclusion, from a unitary and stable view of intelligence to a multidi-

In spite of the fact that more recent research has created an extensive body of evidence on the multiple nature of intelligence and giftedness, most school districts continue to base their gifted programs' identification systems on high general intelligence as measured by group and individual IQ tests and achievement tests.

mensional and dynamic view, and from viewing intelligence measurement as an "objective" enterprise to the inclusion of subjective measures – all of which leads to the recognition that *intelligence must be understood within sociocultural, economic, and, political contexts.*

In conclusion, the latest psychometric studies of intelligence and measurements of intelligence indicate that "standardized tests do not sample all forms of intelligence" (Neisser et al., 1996, p. 97). However, in spite of the fact that more recent research has created an extensive body of evidence on the multiple nature of intelligence and giftedness, most school districts continue to base their gifted programs' identification systems on high general intelligence as measured by group and individual IQ tests and achievement tests. Because these tests cannot and should not be used as the sole determiner of entrance to gifted programs, it is important to know some best practices that offer alternative pathways to gifted program inclusion for CLD students.

Exemplary Identification Practices: A Generic View

A body of literature based on theory, research, and experience suggests the use, or combined use, of certain instruments and procedures for assessing and identifying gifted CLD learners. The following paragraphs provide a sample of those instruments and procedures identified in the literature as effective for assessing and identifying various CLD learners as a group. This discussion of more generic practices will be followed by suggestions for exemplary identification practices specific to Native Americans, African Americans, Hispanics, and Asian Americans.

Establishing a Belief System and Theoretical Base

An absolute precondition for identifying giftedness among CLD learners is the establishment and commitment to a school culture that believes that these youngsters *can be gifted and talented or have giftedness potential.* A school-wide, family, and community belief system, based on the assumption that gifts and talents are distributed as fully among CLD learners as they are among all learners, must permeate the culture of our schools, families, and communities.

Several writers have reached consensus on those exemplary identification practices that should guide the search for giftedness within populations of CLD students (Frasier, 1987; Kitano & Kirby, 1986; Maker & Schiever, 1989; Patton, 1992). For a philosophical and theoretical approach to guide the identification process, the use of expanded views of intelligence and giftedness is recommended. Using models such as those proposed by Sternberg (1985) and Gardner (1983) as well as Renzulli's (1978) three-ring notion of giftedness as a combination of above-average ability, task commitment, and creativity would result in expanded and multidimensional identification approaches.

The use of such inclusive theoretical models would lead naturally to the collection and use of nomination, screening, assessment, and identification data based on multiple criteria and gathered from multiple objective and subjective sources. These data sources would include the use of standardized test results, interview results, case studies, criteria-referenced test results, inventories, teacher recommendations, parent recommendations, community-member and peer recommendations, and the use of student performance and portfolio products.

An absolute precondition for identifying giftedness among CLD learners is the establishment and commitment to a school culture that believes that these youngsters can be gifted and talented or have giftedness potential.

Nominating and Screening: What Teachers and Parents Can Do

Students in gifted programs are generally nominated to these programs by various individuals, most often teachers. Teachers, parents, and family members who have knowledge, understanding, awareness, and appreciation of their own culture and that of "others" are more inclined to recommend that CLD students be nominated to gifted programs. Given the large and pervasive cultural incongruities existing between teachers and students in today's schools, the cultural attitudes held by teachers become critically important and have powerful implications for the nomination and identification process.

Teachers, through their own analysis and development, can choose between being "gatekeepers" of the current condition of disproportionate representation of CLD learners in gifted programs

Given the large and pervasive cultural incongruities existing between teachers and students in today's schools, the cultural attitudes held by teachers become critically important and have powerful implications for the nomination and identification process.

or "gateway" agents who advocate for opening opportunities for these learners. Gateway teachers, working in concert with parents and other family members, represent critical forces in the gifted screening and identification processes.

Spindler and Spindler (1996) point out that teachers are cultural agents and, as such, bring to their interactions with students cultural perceptions and assumptions about students' cultures that can "seriously influence behavior, perceptions of behavior, and communication" (p. 30). They continue by saying that these assumptions and preconceptions are the "starting points of consequences, rewards, punishments, oppositions, and the use of power to coerce, eliminate, damage, and promote" (p. 30).

These cultural assumptions, oftentimes implicitly held by teachers, can serve as powerful mediators to enhance or inhibit the identification of giftedness among CLD learners. It could be argued that, if teachers engaged in some form of "cultural therapy" to become aware and conscious of these underlying processes and subsequently work through them and act upon this "baggage," they could better adjust their attitudes and subsequent actions in order to increase the presence of CLD learners in gifted programs.

Additionally, if teachers and parents advocate for the use of multiple sources of nomination data in the screening process, the representation of CLD learners in gifted programs would be increased. Nomination to gifted programs should be sought from other sources such as support personnel, as well as CLD learners themselves, and from key informants outside the school including extended family members, community representatives, religious leaders, community recreation specialists, librarians, and the like.

The intent of this expanded nomination process is to create the largest net of potential gifted learners as possible from which to assess and identify (Kitano & Kirby, 1986). Further, certain procedures that employ the use of multiple measures in the screening and identification process have been proven to enhance the probability of including CLD students in programs targeted for talent development.

Screening: Checklists, Rating Scales, and Inventories

It is widely understood that the social, cognitive, and affective characteristics of gifted students are generally distinguished from those of nongifted students in nature and kind. On the other hand, some researchers believe that most of the extant, generic characteristics of the gifted are based on a biased European American cultural worldview and that cultural and linguistic diversity often masks giftedness (e.g., Baldwin, 1989; Frasier, 1989; Kitano & Kirby, 1986; Maker & Schiever, 1989; Patton, 1993).

For example, Hilliard (1991), Gay (1978), Patton (1995), and Baldwin (1989) have suggested that African American students have some unique cognitive, social, and affective characteristics that differ from other cultural groups and, therefore, require culturally specific checklists to adequately identify gifted characteristics within African American populations. Tonemah (1987) makes the same argument about Native Americans, Bernal (1989) about Hispanics, and Chen (1989) about Asian Americans.

In a more generic sense, a series of self-report inventories of creativity known as The Group Inventory for Finding Talent (GIFT; Rimm, 1976; Rimm & Davis, 1976, 1980) and The Group Inventory for Finding Interest (GIFFI I and GIFFI II; Davis & Rimm, 1983) were developed for use with individuals from preschool to senior high school. According to Torrance (in press), these inventories are technically sound and contain a breadth of psychometric design that should enhance their use with learners from diverse cultural groups and socioeconomic levels.

Suffice it to say that more CLD learners would be identified for gifted programs if the nomination and screening processes included the use of checklists, rating scales, inventories, interviews, developmental histories, and case studies. A summary of recommended culturally specific checklists, inventories, and rating scales is included later in this chapter.

Suffice it to say that more CLD learners would be identified for gifted programs if the nomination and screening processes included the use of checklists, rating scales, inventories, interviews, developmental histories, and case studies.

Identification

The heavy reliance on the use of standardized intelligence and achievement tests in the gifted identification process, with the exception of certain Asian Americans, has generally not resulted in the proportionate identification for gifted programs of CLD learners. Some standardized instruments, or their adaptations, given their focus on inclusion and an expanded view of intelligence, have been recommended for use with CLD learners. For example, Frasier (1989) has suggested that the Torrance Tests of Creative Thinking (TTCT) are an "unbiased measure of bright black and other minority children (Torrance, 1977, p. 162). Relatedly, she suggested that the use of the Kaufman Assessment Battery for Children (K-ABC; Kaufman & Kaufman, 1983) and the Raven Standard and Progressive Matrices (Raven, 1956) are fair to CLD learners.

Another standardized measure of aptitude, the Matrix Analogies Test, both the expanded and short forms (MAT-EF and MAT-SF), has been normed on a large, national sample of individuals representative of diverse genders, races, ethnicities, socioeconomic status, and geographic regions. It, therefore, contains psychometric dimensions that have the potential of being favorable to CLD learners (Naglieri, 1985). The MAT-EF was used as part of an assessment protocol in Project Mandala, a federally funded Jacob Javits project designed to identify underrepresented, gifted, CLD learners. Studies conducted by Ward, Ward, and Patton (1992) found that a significant number of previously overlooked, gifted, CLD learners were subsequently identified as gifted through the use of the MAT-EF. In fact, the MAT-EF provided a higher estimate of general intellectual ability for a substantial portion of the CLD students in Project Mandala than any other aptitude measures employed in the assessment protocol.

Several other researchers have suggested the use of certain standardized instruments for use with specific cultural groups. These instruments will be discussed later in this chapter. Suffice it to say that, if schools are serious about increasing their numbers of CLD gifted learners and feel tied to standardized instruments, they should select standardized instruments that reflect both an expanded view of intelligence and the school's commitment to include, rather than exclude, CLD learners.

Profile Identification Systems

Most recently, profile approaches have been used in attempts to increase the quality and quantity of identified gifted and talented CLD learners. These approaches have their origins in the earlier matrix approaches advocated and used by Baldwin (1984) and Dabney (1988) and have been reported to be able to increase the number and kinds of CLD learners identified as gifted. Particularly, the work of Frasier (1990) has placed the profile approach at the center of attempts to identify gifted and talented CLD learners.

A major assumption of any profile approach is the embracing of a pluralistic view of giftedness, one that recognizes the existence of multiple domains for the manifestation of gifts and talents (e.g., aptitude, achievement, creativity, and leadership). These matrix approaches have been designed to allow the user to arrange the results of multiple, objective and subjective data sources into a matrix format, so that data from multiple sources can be collected, reviewed, and interpreted before decisions are made about selecting individuals for inclusion in programs for the gifted. While identifying and building on the strengths of learners, a profile system allows for and recognizes the possibility of manifestations of extreme giftedness in one specific domain of intelligence while allowing for average or above-average performance in other domains. Thus, considerations are allowed for the manifestation of an uneven distribution of giftedness across several domains of intelligence.

A profile system allows for and recognizes the possibility of manifestations of extreme giftedness in one specific domain of intelligence while allowing for average or above-average performance in other domains.

More recently, Frasier's development of an assessment-profile approach holds promise for enhancing educators' capacity to discover gifted CLD learners often overlooked by more traditional approaches. The Frasier Talent Assessment Profile (F-TAP; Frasier, 1990) allows users to collect both quantitative and qualitative data from multiple sources on individual, potentially gifted students. The resultant individual "biography," or profile, includes information from which identification and selection decisions can be subsequently made by a team of appropriate professionals. The identification decision is based, then, upon considering multiple and broad areas of indicators of giftedness, or potential giftedness, and allows for withholding identification decisions until all information is collected, profiled, and reviewed (Frasier, 1990).

Intervention Planning and Authentic Assessment Approaches

Several curriculum-based assessment and intervention models have been documented as being useful in increasing the number of CLD learners in programs for the gifted and talented. Based on "dynamic assessment" models advocated by Haywood, Tzuiel, and Vaught (1992) and popularized previously by Feuerstein (1968, 1977), these intervention approaches utilize dynamic measures that identify the learner's responsiveness to instruction through an "iden-

Portfolio and performance assessment models basically ask students "to perform tasks that closely emulate the mental tasks of life" (Archambault, 1992, p. 5).

tification through teaching and intervention" approach (e.g., test, teach, retest). This intervention procedure allows teachers to collect baseline, diagnostic data relative to the learner's display of abilities. These data are then used in the creation of teaching and intervention programs designed to facilitate the learner's development.

Based on this diagnostic information, students are given an opportunity to demonstrate their skills over extended periods of time, enabling them to further refine these skills while program staff refine their judgments about these students' abilities to meet the demands of a gifted program (Johnson, Starnes, Gregory, & Blaylock, 1985). Student responsiveness to differentiated classroom curricula, then, becomes a part of the gifted program selection and intervention paradigm.

Additional alternative assessment approaches to the identification of children, approaches that employ techniques other than pencil-and-paper tests and multiple-choice formats, have recently become popular and offer great potential in the identification of gifted CLD learners. Some promising research and practice emphasize the use of alternative forms of student performance and portfolio assessment to identify exceptional performance and potential (Hadaway & Merek-Schroer, 1992). Portfolio and performance assessment models basically ask students "to perform tasks that closely emulate the mental tasks of life" (Archambault, 1992, p. 5). For more information on portfolio assessment, see Chapter 2.

Portfolio approaches are based upon a systematic observation and data collection of students' products as they engage in authentic learning activities. As Shaklee and Viechnicki (1995) have reported, the portfolio approach represents the purposeful collection of student products gleaned from multiple sources of evidence drawn over extended periods of time. This approach benefits from gathering, simultaneously, assessment and intervention data drawn from the intersection of assessment, curriculum, and instructional applications (Asp, 1992). Dynamic assessment and intervention approaches along with student-portfolio and performance-assessment approaches appropriately connect assessment and identification processes with curriculum and instructional planning and intervention. The application of both approaches, that often employ mediated learning experiences early in the learner's educational career, hold promise in identifying and nurturing the gifts and talent of all CLD learners.

Although teachers are not school psychologists or psychometricians, they are in a position to recommend and influence the identification process. The general suggestions offered thus far and summarized in Table 5.1 should provide them with the knowledge, skills, and attitudes to identify and nurture a wealth of untapped potential in today's schools and society.

Exemplary Identification Practices Unique to Specific Culturally and Linguistically Diverse Learners

This part of the chapter will provide suggestions for using certain techniques, approaches, instruments, and procedures that could be considered unique to specific CLD groups. It is important to remember that, while many cultural similarities and cultural-deep structure features exist within each of the previously identified ethnic groups, not all individuals within a particular group are necessarily alike. There are important intra- and inter-group differences that should be considered in any discussion about CLD students. For example, while Japanese Americans and Chinese Americans are considered a part of the group called "Asian Americans," cultural differences exist within the Japanese group and between the Japanese and Chinese Americans. These dissimilarities result from differences in, to name a few categories, acculturation, heritage, religious practices, child-rearing practices, and sociopolitical factors. This same observation can be made in varying degrees about Native Americans, Hispanics, and African Americans. In short, not all members of one group are the same. The reader is cautioned to be cognizant of the existence of intra- and inter-group differences when reviewing this section of the chapter.

Further, teachers, parents, and others involved in the identification process would be well advised to focus their identification efforts on the strengths that individuals display. One major orga-

It is important to remember that, while many cultural similarities and cultural-deep structure features exist within each of the previously identified ethnic groups, not all individuals within a particular group are necessarily alike.

Table 5.1

Summary of Exemplary Practices in the Identification of Giftedness Among Culturally and Linguistically Diverse Learners

1. Believing is seeing. Work toward the development of a school, home, and community culture that contains a belief system that CLD learners are and can be gifted and talented. This belief system should become the base for the identification of strengths among these learners.

2. Advocate the use of an identification process guided by a knowledge and appreciation of the culture, language, values, and worldviews of CLD learners and their families. This cultural knowledge and awareness should allow teachers to better "connect" with CLD learners and coach them into identifying their own unique gifts and talents.

3. Be alert and responsive to heterogeneity and *intragroup* differences within various CLD groups, in terms of customs, language, child-rearing practices, family structure and dynamics, and religious practices. Distinctive differences can and do exist within the traditional CLD groups and between subpopulations within these groups. For example, within the group called Asian Americans, differences in customs, language, religion, and other areas exist within Vietnamese Americans and among Vietnamese, Chinese, Japanese, Koreans, and so on. The same observation can be made about Hispanics, Native Americans, and African Americans.

4. Ensure the use of a multidimensional, multimodal, dynamic assessment process that employs both qualitative and quantitative data in the collection process.

5. Develop programs in schools, homes, and communities that educate lay persons as to generic behavioral indicators of giftedness and ways in which giftedness is manifested and sometimes masked in different cultures. Help to build school, home, and peer cultures, whereby students view giftedness and talent and their pursuit as a cultural imperative. Seek out "elders" and other informed cultural knowledge brokers to participate in this process.

6. Start your search to identify giftedness among CLD learners in students' early years and continue the process until all potential data is collected. Then look at all the different data in their totality before making a decision. If you are to err, *err in favor of inclusion of the student in a gifted and talented program.*

7. Develop a "try out" program or process that allows these students time and support needed for gifted program selection.

8. Ensure that assessment and identification insights are utilized in curriculum and instruction design and delivery.

nizing theme of the search, screening, and identification process should be to cast all eyes on the strengths learners exhibit both within and outside schools. Oftentimes these learners are unusually strong leaders, have insightful individual skills, or have a creative talent not easily recognized. If teachers and parents look for strengths, they will find them.

Identifying Giftedness Among Native Americans

Native Americans have been variously called Indian and American Indian. The Native American Law Center has 52 legal definitions of Native Americans and reports that 177 different tribes are recognized by the U.S. government (Hirschfelder, 1982). Stereotypical negative perceptions of the abilities of Native Americans have been a major factor contributing to the low number of Native Americans identified as gifted. This naive presumption is the first barrier to be overcome in the identification process.

As with other CLD groups, it is important that the gifted identification process for Native Americans be guided by a knowledge and appreciation of characteristics of their unique culture. Maker and Schiever (1989) have provided an analysis of possible manifestations of absolute aspects of giftedness filtered by certain cultural values associated with the behaviors of Native Americans (see Table 5.2). Additionally, Montgomery (1989) has outlined a process for identifying giftedness among Native Americans that

- Incorporates an understanding of the differential characteristics and diversity that exist within and between various Indian tribes.
- Uses multiple psychometric measures.
- Embraces a definition of giftedness based upon Native American culture.
- Employs naturalistic observations in the screening and referral process.
- Recognizes specific talent of Native Americans, such as problem solving, dance or creative movements, visual arts, and storytelling.

Table 5.3 contains a listing of tribal/cultural perspectives of gifted and talented American Indian students offered by parents and educators of American Indians (Tonemah, 1985).

One major organizing theme of the search, screening, and identification process should be to cast all eyes on the strengths learners exhibit both within and outside schools. Oftentimes these learners are unusually strong leaders, have insightful individual skills, or have a creative talent not easily recognized.

Table 5.2
Interactive Influence of Giftedness Characteristics and the Cultural Values of American Indians

Absolute Aspects of Giftedness Identified in the Literature	Cultural Values Often Identified in the Literature as Characteristic of American Indians	Behavioral Differences Associated With American Indians
Displays unusual sensitivity to expectations and feelings of others	Represents well the collective self, the Tribe	Is a good mediator
Can generate original ideas and solutions		Figures out strategies to help group or team project
Has high level of language development		Communicates effectively the collective idea of tribe
Exhibits idealism, a sense of justice, and advanced levels of moral judgment		Has personal and religious integrity
Displays leadership qualities; is strongly motivated by self-actualization needs		Accepts responsibility and discipline of leadership
Maintains high expectations of self and others		Encourages others to explore and develop abilities while developing own abilities
Exhibits creativity in endeavors	Values traditions, heritage, beliefs	Makes up stories or poems
Retains extraordinary quantity of information, has unusual retentiveness		Recalls old legends about landmarks and the like
Is creative in various areas of endeavor		Reproduces traditional designs or symbols in a variety of media

Note: From *Critical Issues in Gifted Education: Defensible Programs for Cultural and Ethnic Minorities* (p. 78) by C. J. Maker and S. W. Schiever, 1989, Austin, Texas: PRO-ED. Copyright 1989 PRO-ED. Adapted with permission.

Identifying Giftedness Among African Americans

The identification of giftedness among African Americans has been a complex and perplexing challenge. Much of the early research and practice reflected a strong inclination to associate African American cultural issues with socioeconomic class issues; thus, the historical focus has been on their "disadvantagement" (Baldwin, Gear, & Lucito, 1978; Frasier, 1987; Gay, 1978; Torrance, 1977). For example, unlike the literature focusing on the culture of Hispanics, Asian Americans, or Native Americans, much of the extant literature in gifted education related to African Americans reflects a gifted, "disadvantaged" analysis, rather than a gifted African American cultural analysis. This deficit-centered analysis, which permeates the African American gifted education and human science research and literature base, has been an inhibiting factor in the development of a culturally appropriate and progressive knowledge base upon which to build gifted identification and intervention systems.

However, a host of African American researchers has argued for the development of assessment and identification systems grounded in the unique worldview, values, cultures, and behaviors of Americans of African descent (Frasier, 1990; Gay, 1978; Hilliard, 1991; Patton, 1992; Shade, 1978). The focus of these models is on telling the stories of the strengths, resilience, and life-enhancing qualities embedded in African American culture. As an example, my analysis (Patton, 1992) of classical African-American-oriented philosophical worldviews and theoretical orientations offers some African-centered cultural characteristics that could guide theory development and practice relative to the identification of giftedness among African Americans.

As illustrated in Table 5.4, when identifying giftedness among African Americans, it is important to consider context, synthetical thinking versus analytical thinking, "doing" something versus impassivity, and feelings and human social content. Additionally, collective or group action versus individual behavior is valued in the African tradition, and emotions and affect are important. If identification systems incorporated these and other aspects of African American culture, more African American learners would be labeled and treated as gifted.

Table 5.3
Characteristics for Identifying
Gifted American Indian Students

Acquired Skills

Learning skills

Language/communication skills

Technological skills

*Tribal/Cultural
Understanding*

Knowledge of ceremonies

Knowledge of tribal traditions

Knowledge of tribes

Aesthetic Qualities

Demonstrated visual art talent

Demonstrated performing art talent

Creative expression

Indian art(s) talent

Personal/Human Qualities

High intelligence

Vision, inquisitiveness, intuition

Creativity

Individualism, self-discipline

Leadership

Athletic prowess, coordination, dexterity

Respect for elders

Note: From *Tribal-Cultural Perspective of Gifted and Talentedness* by S. Tonemah, 1985, An unpublished manuscript available from D. Montgomery, Elmhurst School, Oklahoma City, OK. Copyright 1985 by S. Tonemah. Reprinted with permission.

Table 5.4

Some African-American-Oriented
Philosophical Worldviews and Theoretical Orientations

Metaphysics	*Axiology*	*Epistemology*
Use of a Holistic View of Reality	*Importance of Person-to-Person Interaction*	*Affective Orientation*
The individual tends to engage in synthetical and contextual thinking. Emphasis is placed on viewing the "whole" field and then understanding the interconnectedness of what might seem to be disparate parts of the field.	The individual is committed to developing strong *social* bonds that often transcend individual privileges. Communal existence is paramount to individual reality. Interpersonal relations and leadership skills are valued parts of this belief system.	The individual places emphasis on emotions and feelings and is sensitive to *emotional* cues. The tendency for emotional expressiveness is usually apparent. Connecting the affective with cognitive and psychomotor ways of knowing is important.

Note: The information obtained in the metaphysics and axiology sections of this table is drawn from the philosophical and conceptual works of Dixon (1976), Nichols (1976), Maurier (1979), and Nobles (1991). Information in the epistemology section is drawn from these same authors and the theoretical work of Boykin (1983).

Effective identification methods include the use of a combination of measures, both standardized and nonstandardized, that assess creativity, achievement, leadership, and nonverbal ability.

Additionally, Gay (1978), Shade (1978), and Baldwin (1984) developed checklists for evaluating behavioral manifestations of giftedness in African American learners. Frasier (1989), as previously discussed, suggested the use of an identification scheme to increase the number of African Americans identified as gifted. Their schemata place heavy reliance on the use of multiple qualitative and quantitative data sources in the nomination, screening, assessment, and selection processes. Furthermore, Fitz-Gibbon (1975) developed a highly effective method to adapt the administration and analysis of results of conventional intelligence and achievement tests; this method emphasizes inclusion and delayed judgment in the identification process.

Often, effective identification methods include the use of a combination of measures, both standardized and nonstandardized, that assess creativity, achievement, leadership, and nonverbal ability. As previously mentioned, such measures include the Torrance Tests of Creative Thinking (TTCT), the Kaufman Assessment Battery for Children (K-ABC), and the Raven Standard and Advance Progressive Matrices. Additionally, the Baldwin Identification Matrix (BIM; Baldwin, 1984) and the Frasier Talent Assessment Profile (F-TAP; Frasier, 1990) have proven to be effective procedures for increasing the representation of African Americans in gifted programs.

Also previously mentioned, several curriculum-based assessment and intervention models have been documented as being useful in increasing the inclusion of African-American learners in programs for the gifted and talented. Research by Johnson et al. (1985) describing the assessment system employed by the Program for Assessment, Diagnosis, and Intervention (PADI) found the system effective in identifying large number of African American students for gifted programs. Additionally, the previously discussed performance and portfolio assessment and intervention approaches (see also Chapter 2) have proven to be particularly effective in increasing the number of African American learners as gifted. The reader is encouraged to review all of these references for more details related to identification techniques and practices effective for African Americans.

Identifying Giftedness Among Hispanic Americans

Hispanic is a term primarily defined by heritage and generally refers to Mexican Americans or Chicanos, Puerto Ricans, Central Americans, South Americans, and Cubans. Identifying giftedness within these populations requires the inclusion and consideration of the various cultural values, worldviews, language, and characteristics in the determination of the gifted definition and the nomination, assessment, screening and identification processes. Giftedness among Hispanic students is manifested in cognitive, affective, and social behaviors consistent with all gifted students and, at the same time, reflective of behaviors peculiar to Hispanic culture. As Leung (1981) and Maker and Schiever (1989) point out, Hispanic culture serves as a context through which the absolute characteristics of giftedness are filtered and can be more effectively identified.

Table 5.5 provides a schemata for observing the interactive influence of absolute characteristics of giftedness, certain cultural values of Hispanics, and behavioral differences. Relatedly, Perrine (1989) has described a " situational identification program," entitled the *Screening and Instructional Program*, that has been used successfully in East Los Angeles. Using the perspective outlined in Table 5.5, the program employs an identification system for potentially gifted Hispanics that incorporates search, instruction, and dynamic-evaluation processes. Initially, program staffers disseminated throughout the Los Angeles School District listings of social, intellectual, and linguistic characteristics of gifted students. This constituted the search component of the identification process.

Checklists were used by trained school personnel to observe and record specific student behaviors that were later analyzed. Potentially gifted students were then clustered in regular classrooms for instruction and provided special nurturance designed to "unearth" this giftedness. Evaluation of the students' responses to the instruction was a continuing process that reflected the instructional and dynamic evaluation component of the identification system (Perrine, 1989). Instruction was then designed to complement and build upon the knowledge base the Hispanic students brought to the classroom.

Instruction must capitalize and build upon the strengths that CLD students bring with them to the schools.

Perrine (1989) believes that this program created a community dynamic that proved the existence of gifted Hispanic students in the East Los Angeles community. The absolute prerequisite that instruction must capitalize and build upon – and one emphasized in this program – is the strengths that CLD students bring with them to the schools.

Identifying Giftedness Among Asian Americans

The major Asian American groups in the United States are Japanese Americans, Chinese Americans, Vietnamese Americans, and Korean Americans. Many first- and second-generation offsprings of Asian parents who came to the United States in the early to mid 1900s have been quite successful in schools. In fact, Chen and Goon (1978) found that gifted incidence rates for Asian Americans is higher than normally would be expected in the general population.

Consideration of the unique behaviors of Asian American students should be employed in the identification process. Table 5.6 provides a model for factoring into the gifted definition and identification process certain cultural characteristics and behavioral differences of Asian Americans. Chen (1989) and Kitano (1989) have provided similar designs for the identification of giftedness among Asian American learners. This process, according to both authors, requires a multidimensional approach that includes the previously mentioned process and curriculum-based assessment and that may require adaptations based on students' learning styles. Both caution teachers to attend to cultural differences in the screening and evaluation process. For example, they indicate that these learners might exhibit giftedness more often in quiet, independent work settings rather than in social settings. Additionally, Chen (1989) observed that teachers, rather than emphasizing the attainment of information, should be cognizant of the learning processes and styles and behavioral indicators used by the students, such as insight, transformational thinking, rapid learning rate, making associations, analyzing patterns, self-discipline, intensity, and sustained motivation and interest.

Table 5.5
Interactive Influence of Giftedness Characteristics
and the Cultural Values of Hispanics

Absolute Aspects of Giftedness Identified in the Literature	Cultural Values Often Identified in the Literature as Characteristic of Hispanics	Behavioral Differences Associated with Hispanics
Displays high level of verbal ability	Uses traditional language of family	Communicates fluently with peers and within community, even if using nonstandard English
Exhibits emotional depth and intensity	Has abrazo, a physical or spiritual index of personal support	Requires touching, eye contact, feeling of support to achieve maximum academic productivity
Shows unusual sensitivity to feelings and expectations of others	Participates in family structure and dynamics, including male dominance	Displays personal initiative and independent thought; verbal aggressiveness is often inhibited in females
Conceptualizes solutions to social and environmental problems	Values nuclear and extended family closeness	Often assumes responsibility for family and/or younger siblings
Displays unusual retentiveness; has unusual capacity for processing information	Takes pride in traditional culture	Adapts to successful functioning in two cultures
Exhibits leadership qualities	Is collaborative rather than competitive	Accomplishes more and works better in small groups than individually

Note: From *Critical Issues in Gifted Education: Defensible Programs for Cultural and Ethnic Minorities* (p. 4) by C. J. Maker and S. W. Schiever, 1989, Austin, Texas: PRO-ED, Inc. Copyright 1989 PRO-ED. Reprinted with permission.

Table 5.6
Interactive Influence of Giftedness Characteristics and the Cultural Values of Asians

Absolute Aspects of Giftedness Identified in the Literature	Cultural Values Often Identified in the Literature as Characteristic of Asians	Behavioral Differences Associated with Asians
Displays a strong need for consistency between abstract values	Has arugama or akirame (mature self-control or resignation)	Displays passivity, lack of assertiveness
Holds high expectations of self	Acts on Confucianist ethic: people can be improved by proper effort and instruction	Shows high academic orientation and achievement
Is unusually sensitive to expectations and feelings of others	Values family honor and tradition; takes personal responsibility	Has self-discipline, self-motivation; shows preference for structure and defined limits
Shows signs of perfectionism	Displays conformity, correctness, respect for and obedience to authority	Exhibits patience and willingness for drill and rote exercises; prefers decreased risk taking and creative expression
Exhibits persistent, goal-directed behavior	Values educational achievement and the work ethic	Concentrates and persists on academic tasks

Note: From *Critical Issues in Gifted Education: Defensible Programs for Cultural and Ethnic Minorities* (p. 152) by C. J. Maker and S. W. Schiever, 1989, Austin, Texas: PRO-ED, Inc. Copyright 1989 by PRO-ED. Reprinted with permission.

Conclusion

Gifted CLD learners, except for certain Asian American populations, are often overlooked for gifted programs and, as a result, are grossly underrepresented in gifted and talented programs. Many researchers and practitioners have spent much time and energy in identifying causes of this underrepresentation. Causative factors have ranged from the overreliance on standardized measures, especially intelligence tests, to considering cultural factors in the screening, assessment, and identification process. Solutions to this educational, social, political, and economic problem have been minuscule, in comparison to problem identification.

Teachers are at the heart of solutions. If they examine their own cultural biases and reach a healthy comfort level with their cultural selves, it is very likely that they will be better able to understand, appreciate, and interact with the cultures of others, especially those students who have not been on "center stage." With this enhanced awareness, teachers should be better equipped to operate from a belief system and advocacy perspective that inspires CLD learners to unearth their already existing unique talents and gifts. Furthermore, this liberation should enhance teachers' own knowledge, skills, and attitudes related to identifying these students' gifts and subsequently nurturing their talents. Finally, if teachers become more knowledgeable of practices that are better able to identify the gifts and talents of CLD learners, the challenge of underrepresentation will be met.

References

Archambault, F. X. (1992). *Alternative assessment and the evaluation of programs for the gifted and talented.* Unpublished manuscript. University of Connecticut, National Research Center on the Gifted and Talented, Storrs.

Asp, E. (1992, April). *Portfolio as evaluation.* Presentation at the Primary Teacher Institute, Kent State University, Kent, OH.

Baldwin, A. Y. (1984). *The Baldwin Identification Matrix 2 for the identification of the gifted and talented: A handbook for its use.* New York: Trillium Press.

Baldwin, A. Y. (1989). The purpose of education for gifted Black students. In C. J. Maker & S. W. Schiever (Eds.), *Critical issues in gifted education: Defensible programs for cultural and ethnic minorities* (Vol. 2, pp. 237-245). Austin, TX: PRO-ED.

Baldwin, A. Y., Gear, G. H., & Lucito, L. J. (Eds.). (1978). *Educational planning for the gifted: Overcoming cultural, geographic, and socioeconomic barriers.* Reston, VA: The Council for Exceptional Children.

Bernal, E. M. (1989). "Pluralism and power": Dare we reform education of the gifted along these lines. In C. J. Maker & S. W. Schiever (Eds.), *Critical issues in gifted education: Defensible programs for cultural and ethnic minorities* (Vol. 2, pp. 34-36). Austin, TX: PRO-ED.

Boykin, A. W. (1983). The academic performance of Afro-American children. In J. Spence (Ed.), *Achievement and achievement motives* (pp. 321-371). San Francisco: W.H. Freeman.

Chen, J. (1989). Identification of gifted Asian-American students. In C. J. Maker & S. W. Schiever (Eds.), *Critical issues in gifted education: Defensible programs for cultural and ethnic minorities* (Vol. 2, pp. 154-162). Austin, TX: PRO-ED.

Chen, J., & Goon, S. (1978). Recognition of the gifted from among disadvantaged Asian children. *Gifted Child Quarterly, 20,* 157-164.

Dabney, M. (1988). An alternative model for identification of potentially gifted students: A case study. In R. L. Jones (Ed.), *Psychoeducational assessment of minority group children: A casebook* (pp. 273-294). Berkeley, CA: Cobb & Henry.

Davis, G. A., & Rimm, S. (1983). Group Inventory for Finding Interest (GIFFI) I and II: Instruments for identifying creative potential in the junior and senior high school. *Journal of Creative Behavior, 6,* 50-57.

Dixon, V. J. (1976). World views and research methodology. In L. M. King, V. J. Dixon, & W. W. Nobles (Eds.), *African philosophy: Assumptions and paradigms for research on Black persons* (pp. 51-102). Los Angeles: Fanon Center Publication.

Feuerstein, R. (1968). *The learning potential of assessment device: A new method for assessing modifiability of the cognitive functioning of socioculturally disadvantaged adolescents.* Unpublished manuscript, Israel Foundation Trustees, Tel Aviv.

Feuerstein, R. (1977). Mediated learning experience: A theoretical basis for cognitive human modifiability during adolescence. *Research to practice in mental retardation: Proceedings of the 4th Congress of IASMD: Vol. 2. Education and training* (pp. 105-116). Baltimore: University Park Press.

Fitz-Gibbon, C. T. (1975). The identification of mentally gifted "disadvantaged" students at the eighth grade level. *Journal of Negro Education, 43*(1), 53-66.

Frasier, M. (1987). The identification of gifted Black students: Developing new perspectives. *Journal for the Education of the Gifted, 10*(3), 155-180.

Frasier, M. (1989). Identification of gifted Black students: Developing new perspectives. In C. J. Maker & S. W. Schiever (Eds.), *Critical issues in gifted education: Defensible programs for cultural and ethnic minorities* (Vol. 2, pp. 213-325). Austin, TX: PRO-ED.

Frasier, M. (1990, April). *The equitable identification of gifted and talented children.* Paper presented at the annual meeting of the American Educational Research Association, Boston.

Gardner, H. (1983). *Frames of mind.* New York: Basic Books.

Gay, J. E. (1978). A proposed plan for identifying Black gifted children. *Gifted Child Quarterly, 22*(3), 353-360.

Gould, S. J. (1981). *The mismeasure of man.* New York: Norton.

Hadaway, N., & Merek-Schroer, M. (1992). Multidimensional assessment of the gifted minority student. *Roeper Review, 15*(2), 73-77.

Haywood, H. C., Tzuiel, D., & Vaught, S. (1992). Psychoeducational assessment from a transactional perspective. In H. C. Haywood & D. Tzuriel (Eds.), *Interactive assessment* (pp. 38-63). New York: Springer.

Hilliard, A. G. (1991). *Testing African American students.* Morristown, NJ: Aaron Press.

Hirschfelder, O. (1982). *American Indian stereotypes in the world of children.* Metuchen, NJ: Scarecrow Press.

Johnson, S. T., Starnes, W. T., Gregory, D., & Blaylock, A. (1985). Program of assessment, diagnosis, and instruction (PADI): Identifying and nurturing potentially gifted and talented minority students. *The Journal of Negro Education, 54*(3), 416-430.

Kaufman, A., & Kaufman, N. (1983). *Kaufman assessment battery for children (K-ABC).* Circle Pines, MN: American Guidance Service.

Kitano, M. K. (1989). Critique of "Identification of Gifted Asian-American Students." In C. J. Maker & S. W. Schiever (Eds.), *Critical issues in gifted education: Defensible programs for cultural and ethnic minorities* (Vol. 2, pp. 163-168). Austin, TX: PRO-ED.

Kitano, M. K., & Kirby, D. F. (1986). *Gifted education: A comprehensive view.* Boston: Little, Brown.

Leung, E. K. (1981, February). *The identification and social problems of gifted bilingual-bicultural children.* Paper presented at The Council for Exceptional Children Conference on the Exceptional Bilingual Child. (ERIC Document Reproduction Service No. ED 203 653)

Maker, C. J., & Schiever, S. W. (Eds.). (1989). *Critical issues in gifted education: Defensible programs for cultural and ethnic minorities* (Vol. 2). Austin, TX: PRO-ED.

Maurier, H. (1979). Do we have an African philosophy? In R. A. Wright (Ed.), *African philosophy: An introduction* (M. McDevitt, Trans.; pp. 1-17). Washington, DC: University of America Press.

Montgomery, D. M. (1989). Identification of giftedness among American Indian people. In C. J. Maker & S. W. Schiever (Eds.), *Critical issues in gifted education: Defensible programs for cultural and ethnic minorities* (Vol. 2, pp. 79-90). Austin, TX: PRO-ED.

Naglieri, J. A. (1985). *Matrix Analogies Test, Short Form and Expanded Form.* San Antonio, TX: Psychological Corp.

Neisser, U., Boodoo, G., Bouchard, T. J., Jr., Boykin, A. W., Brody, N., Ceci, S. J., Halpern, D. F., Loehlin, J. C., Perloff, R., Sternberg, R. J., & Urbina, S. (1996). Intelligence: Knowns and unknowns. *American Psychologist, 51*(2), 77-101.

Nichols, E. J. (1976). *The philosophical aspects of cultural difference.* Unpublished table, University of Ibadan, Nigeria.

Nobles, W. W. (1991). African philosophy: Foundations for Black psychology. In R. L. Jones (Ed.), *Black psychology* (pp. 47-63). Berkeley, CA: Cobb & Henry.

Patton, J. M. (1992). Assessment and identification of African American learners with gifts and talents. *Exceptional Children, 59,* 150-159.

Patton, J. M. (1993). Psychoeducational assessment of gifted and talented African Americans. In J. H. Stanfield II & R. M. Dennis (Eds.), *Race and ethnicity in research methods* (pp. 198- 206). Newbury, CA: Sage.

Patton, J. M. (1995). Identifying and transforming the potential of young, gifted African Americans: A clarion call for action. In B. A. Ford, F. E. Obiakor, & J. M. Patton, *Effective education of African American exceptional learners: New perspectives* (pp. 27-67). Austin, TX: PRO-ED.

Perrine, J. (1989). Situational identification of gifted Hispanic students. In C. J. Maker & S. W. Schiever (Eds.), *Critical issues in gifted education: Defensible programs for cultural and ethnic minorities* (Vol. 2, pp. 1-18). Austin, TX: PRO-ED.

Raven, J. (1956). *Progressive matrices.* London: H. D. Lewis.

Renzulli, J. S. (1978). "What makes giftedness?" Reexamining a definition. *Phi Delta Kappan, 60,* 180-184; 261.

Richert, E. S. (1987). Rampant problems and promising practices in the identification of disadvantaged gifted children. *Gifted Child Quarterly, 31,* 149-164.

Rimm, S. (1976). *GIFT: Group Inventory for Finding Talent.* Watertown, WI: Educational Assessment Service.

Rimm, S., & Davis, G. A. (1976). GIFT: An instrument for the identification of creativity. *Journal of Creative Behavior, 10,* 178-182.

Rimm, S., & Davis, G. A. (1980). Five years of international research with GIFT: An instrument for the identification of creativity. *Journal of Creative Behavior, 14,* 35-46.

Shade, B. J. (1978). Social-psychological traits of achieving Black children. *The Negro Educational Review, 29,* 80-86.

Shaklee, B. D., & Viechnicki, K. J. (1995). A qualitative approach to portfolios: The Early Assessment for Exceptional Potential Model. *Journal for the Education of the Gifted, 18*(2), 156-170.

Spindler, G., & Spindler, L. (1996). *Pathways to cultural awareness.* Thousand Oaks, CA: Corwin Press.

Sternberg, R. (1985). *Beyond I. Q.* Cambridge, MA: Cambridge University Press.

Sternberg, R. (1991). Giftedness according to the triarchic theory of human intelligence. In N. Colangelo & G. A. Davis (Eds.), *Handbook of gifted education* (pp. 45-53). Boston: Allyn & Bacon.

Tonemah, S. (1985). *Tribal-cultural perspective of gifted and talentedness.* Unpublished manuscript. (Available from D. Montgomery. Elmhurst School, Oklahoma City, OK)

Tonemah, S. (1987). Assessing American Indian gifted and talented students' abilities. *Journal for the Education of the Gifted, 10*(3), 181-194.

Torrance, E. P. (1977). *Discovery and nurturance of giftedness in the culturally different.* Reston, VA: The Council for Exceptional Children.

Torrance, E. P (in press). *The blazing drive: The creative personality.* Buffalo, NY: Bearly.

Ward, T., Ward, S., & Patton, J. M. (1992, April). *An analysis of the utility of the Matrix Analogies Test with at-risk gifted learners.* Paper presented at the annual meeting of the American Educational Research Association, San Francisco.

Weinberg, R. (1989). Intelligence and IQ: Landmark issues and great debates, *American Psychologist 44*(2), 98-104.

Zappia, I. A. (1989). Identification of gifted Hispanic students: A multidimensional view. In C. J. Maker & S. W. Schiever (Eds.), *Critical issues in gifted education: Defensible programs for cultural and ethnic minorities* (Vol. 2, pp. 19-26). Austin, TX: PRO-ED.

6 Disproportionate Representation: Current Issues and Future Directions

Grace Zamora-Durán
The Council for Exceptional Children

Alfredo J. Artiles
University of California, Los Angeles

The disproportionate representation of culturally and linguistically diverse (CLD) students in special and gifted education programs has long challenged educators across the nation. The many complexities that contribute to disproportionate representation further complicate the analysis of this problem (Artiles & Trent, 1994). As noted repeatedly throughout the chapters in this book, the various contributing factors to disproportionate representation cannot be identified simply nor in isolation.

The essence of the disproportionate representation problem is not whether the right "quota or proportion" of CLD students is placed in special and gifted education programs. Rather, the substance of the disproportionality problem resides in the instances of inappropriate placement decisions for CLD students which deter them from making timely educational progress. In the case of placement in special education programs, concern has been expressed about false positives, that is, about CLD students who are mistakenly thought to have a disabling condition, which results in inappropriate special education placement. There are also instances in which CLD students need to be placed in gifted education programs to develop their potential but such placement does not occur.

These inappropriate placement decisions arise through a myriad of factors, some of which are related to flawed systemic prac-

The essence of the disproportionate representation problem is not whether the right "quota or proportion" of CLD students is placed in special and gifted education programs. Rather, the substance of the disproportionality problem resides in the instances of inappropriate placement decisions for CLD students which deter them from making timely educational progress.

Educators and related services personnel need to understand that there are important inter- as well as intra-group differences. This awareness will help them to be sensitive not only to cultural differences between distinct ethnic or linguistic groups but also to variations within each of these groups.

tices and procedures and personnel issues. Specifically, educators and related services personnel need to understand that there are important inter- as well as intra-group differences. This awareness will help them to be sensitive not only to cultural differences between distinct ethnic or linguistic groups but also to variations within each of these groups. Similarly, teachers and other related personnel must be knowledgeable about basic information regarding cultural diversity and education, for example, how sociocultural variables influence development and learning. In turn, this knowledge will allow professionals to make necessary adaptations in their perceptions of, attitudes toward, and practices with CLD students so that these students experience academic success.

Although many of the aforementioned factors cannot be changed overnight, there are practices within educators' immediate control that can be altered to ensure that disproportionate representation does not occur at the rate it has in the past. This chapter highlights important aspects addressed in earlier chapters which educators can use to enhance the educational opportunities and outcomes of CLD students.

Assessment

Throughout this book, chapter authors recommend identification and assessment practices that will result in a decreased incidence of disproportionate representation of CLD students in special and gifted education programs. Implementing these recommendations will help ensure that students from CLD populations will be appropriately identified and assessed for placement decisions in special and gifted education programs.

Chapter 2 focuses on assessment issues. Rueda emphasizes the importance of going beyond the traditional standardized instruments and incorporating performance assessment measures in natural settings to gain a more comprehensive view of students' abilities. Performance assessment has received increasing attention in the special education field (e.g., Tindal & Marston, 1996). However, discussions and analyses about the use of these assessment procedures with CLD students are virtually nonexistent. Some of Rueda's points include

- New forms of assessment focus on learning processes as well as final products and on tasks which require constructing meaning rather than recalling isolated bits of information.

- Performance-based measures engage students in real-world tasks that produce useful instructional information for teachers.

- Portfolio assessment, a type of performance-based measure, is a collection of students' work over time that provides valuable information for designing instruction.

- Performance and portfolio assessment principles ensure that the process provides useful instructional and student-learning information for teachers.

- Portfolios can be used across settings to achieve various objectives, for example, accommodating differences more effectively, tapping students' background knowledge, documenting higher order thinking processes and outcomes, and involving the family and community in students' education.

- Educators must be aware of their biases regarding teaching, learning, and student differences; make necessary adjustments to their beliefs; and gauge their adeptness at effectively incorporating portfolio assessment principles and techniques within their daily routines.

Behavior Differences

The chapter on behavior differences versus behavior disorders addresses the important role that culture and life experiences within one's culture play in shaping behavioral responses to varying situations. Student behaviors should be understood as embedded in systems of cultural beliefs, assumptions, expectations, and meanings (Trent & Artiles, 1995). Thus, "normal behavior" must be understood as situated in the particular cultural systems in which people's actions are observed. Unfortunately, educators too often make decisions about CLD students' behaviors from the educator's own cultural vantage point without consideration of the cultural meanings that such behaviors may have for students. In Chapter 3, Ishii-Jordan addresses varying styles of behavior that are consistent among certain ethnic groups. Some of the points raised in her chapter include

- Inter- and intra-group general characteristics or themes are common among certain cultural groups and should be considered before making final determinations about a student's response to learning situations or experiences.

- Individual differences far outweigh any general characteristics used to describe groups of people, for example, socioeconomic, educational, acculturational, generational.

- Considerations should be made regarding identification of CLD students including the definition of SED, appropriate assessment, and links between behavior and culture and between behavior and language.

- An array of intervention tactics should be available for positive results; currently, many school systems do not effectively address nor recognize the underlying cultural meanings of student behaviors classified as negative.

- Teachers' beliefs and interpretations of students' behavior have a significant impact on students' behavioral responses.

- Training and development programs must incorporate opportunities for educators to become culturally competent in knowledge and practice.

- Change must occur within assessment, training, and intervention to effectively deal with CLD students who manifest behaviors that may be identified as disordered.

Language

The chapter on language (# 4) describes four categories of communicative competence to consider when evaluating language proficiency. Disproportionate representation of CLD learners in special education programs, especially students who speak a language other than English, can be decreased if teachers learn to view language acquisition as a process situated in sociocultural contexts and to focus on meaningful communication as the intent of language. Important points raised by Zamora-Durán and Reyes include

- Classroom observations are imperative when making determinations about students' true levels of language proficiency.

- A comprehensive view of language includes grammatical, sociolinguistic, discourse, and strategic competencies.

- When teachers focus on language skills and on indicators within each of the competencies that reflect growth or progress, decisions can be made to enhance instruction.

- The usefulness of classroom observation measures heavily depend on teacher input; therefore, teachers must be aware of their cultural assumptions, beliefs, and attitudes regarding second-language learners and learning.

Giftedness

Underrepresentation of CLD students in gifted and talented programs has challenged educators for many years. To correct this imbalance, many researchers and practitioners point to the need to enhance the notion of giftedness so that it transcends narrow definitions which overemphasize the role of intelligence as operationalized in standardized scales. In Chapter 5, Patton reviews information indicating the low enrollment of CLD students in gifted programs and offers recommendations for increasing these numbers. Some of the other points raised in this chapter include

- Standardized intelligence tests do not effectively measure an individual's intelligence because intelligence is multidimensional and needs to be assessed within sociocultural and political contexts.

- Belief systems among school personnel need to reflect the notion that gifts and talents are equally distributed among all students, including CLD students.

- The implementation of expanded nomination systems creates a large net of potentially gifted CLD learners who can be assessed further and identified.

- The use of multiple assessment instruments and methods facilitate the identification of giftedness among CLD populations.

- Inter- and intra-group differences, specifically learning preferences and behavioral responses, must be considered in making decisions and determinations about giftedness among CLD students.

Conclusion

This volume focuses on potential solutions to address the disproportionate representation of CLD students in special and gifted education programs. Contributors address three central domains of CLD students' functioning, namely behavior, language, and outstanding performance (as defined in giftedness). In addition, contributors also offered alternative procedures to assess CLD student learning – indeed a central task in educators' daily work.

Three important conclusions can be drawn from the preceding chapters. First, as has been documented elsewhere (Artiles, Trent, & Kuan, in press), research on CLD students is alarmingly scarce. This important gap must be addressed by research funding agencies and institutions as well as by the community of researchers. It is imperative that special and general educators conduct more research to understand the plight of CLD students.

Second, contributors emphasize the need to transcend simplistic views of culture and cultural differences. Too often, researchers and practitioners have equated culture and cultural differences with ethnicity and race while they have disregarded the critical mediating roles of cultural beliefs and values (Artiles & Trent, in press b; Keogh, Gallimore, & Weisner, in press). In this vein, volume contributors consistently warn about the need to take into account within- and between-group variations. Future research and intervention efforts must keep this important issue in mind to enhance educators' understanding of the complex developmental and learning processes of CLD students.

Third, beliefs held by teachers and related services personnel about CLD students emerged as a theme. These beliefs are woven in assessment decisions, perceptions of students' behaviors, attitudes toward students' gifts and talents or lack thereof, and interpretations of students' language abilities and disabilities. The literature on teacher beliefs in general education emphasizes the importance of self-reflection and self-evaluation. Professionals must understand the influence that their perceptions and attitudes have on students' classroom achievement. Teacher education programs must teach prospective educators to identify, and in some cases alter, their beliefs. Teacher educators should also help prospective teachers to become aware of the importance and impact that their beliefs have on student progress and on educational placements and outcomes. Unfortunately, although interest is increasing in this area, little is currently known about how to best prepare teachers to teach CLD students in special education (Artiles & Trent, in press a). Indeed, more systematic efforts to enhance the knowledge base in this domain are necessary.

The chapters in this book are a first step in addressing the disproportionate representation of CLD students in special and gifted education programs. Although the ideas presented here do not represent an exhaustive list of solutions, we hope they will incite readers to apply some of the ideas in their work and to continue enriching the emerging knowledge base in this area of study.

Professionals must understand the influence that their perceptions and attitudes have on students' classroom achievement.

References

Artiles, A. J., & Trent, S. C. (1994). Overrepresentation of minority students in special education: A continuing debate. *The Journal of Special Education, 27,* 410-437.

Artiles, A. J., & Trent, S. C. (in press a). Forging a research program on multicultural preservice teacher education: A proposed analytic scheme. In J. W. Lloyd, E. Kameenui, & D. Chard (Eds.), *Educating students with disabilities.* Hillsdale, NJ: Lawrence Erlbaum.

Artiles, A. J., & Trent, S. C. (in press b). The knowledge base on culturally diverse students with learning disabilities: The need to enrich learning disabilities research with a sociocultural perspective. *Learning Disabilities Research & Practice.*

Artiles, A. J., Trent, S. C., & Kuan, L. A. (in press). Learning disabilities research on ethnic minority students: An analysis of 22 years of studies published in selected refereed journals. *Learning Disabilities Research & Practice.*

Keogh, B., Gallimore, R., & Weisner, T. (in press). A sociocultural perspective on learning and learning disabilities. *Learning Disabilities Research & Practice.*

Tindal, G., & Marston, D. (1996). Technical adequacy of alternative reading measures as performance assessments. *Exceptionality, 6,* 201-230.

Trent, S. C., & Artiles, A. J. (1995). Serving culturally diverse students with behavior disorders: Broadening current perspectives. In J. M. Kauffman, J. W. Lloyd, T. A., Astuto, & D. P. Hallahan (Eds.), *Issues in the educational placement of pupils with emotional or behavioral disorders* (pp. 215-249). Hillsdale, NJ: Lawrence Erlbaum Associates.

About the Authors

Alfredo J. Artiles

ALFREDO J. ARTILES is Assistant Professor at the UCLA Graduate School of Education and Information Studies. With a Ph.D. from the University of Virginia, Dr. Artiles is currently a Postdoctoral Fellow at the National Center of Minority Research in Special Education (COMRISE). Dr. Artiles's scholarly interests are in issues in the education of culturally diverse learners in general and special education and international/comparative special education. His current research focuses on (a) the disproportionate representation of culturally diverse students in special education programs, (b) teacher learning in multicultural educational contexts, and (c) equity issues in special education reforms around the world. He serves on the editorial boards of several specialized journals including *Educational Research Quarterly, Exceptional Children,* and *Multiple Voices.* Dr. Artiles has worked as a consultant and made presentations at professional conferences in the U.S.A., Latin America, Europe, and Africa.

Sharon R. Ishii-Jordan

SHARON R. ISHII-JORDAN is an assistant professor in the Department of Special Education and Communication Disorders at the University of Nebraska-Lincoln. She received her Ph.D. from the University of Nebraska-Lincoln in 1993. She teaches courses related to secondary special education methods, strategies for students with special needs in regular secondary classrooms, cultural diversity and human relations, and special education issues for administrators. Her research has examined cultural and language concerns among students with emotional/behavioral disorders and inclusive training in preservice teacher development.

James M. Patton

JAMES M. PATTON is Professor of Special Education and Associate Dean of Academic Programs at the College of William and Mary of Virginia. He previously directed Project Mandala, a federally funded research and development project aimed at identifying and serving selected students and their families who exhibit at-risk and at-promise characteristics. His major research interests include the educational and psychosocial development of African Americans, particularly those with gifts and talents; ways to enhance the development of African American males; and analysis of policies affecting people of color and those from low socioeconomic circumstances. His funded grants total approximately $4.5 million.

Elba I. Reyes

ELBA I. REYES is Assistant Professor at the University of Arizona and is the multicultural specialist in the Department of Special Education and Rehabilitation. Dr. Reyes has been in the field of education for 20 years serving culturally and linguistically diverse populations in general education and special education, including teaching training and staff development. Her research interests focus on multicultural populations with special needs and ways that their classroom settings influence language development and learning.

Robert Rueda

ROBERT RUEDA is Professor and Chairperson of the Division of Educational Psychology and Technology in the School of Education at the University of Southern California (USC), Los Angeles. He also teaches in the Language, Literacy, and Learning Program. He received his Ph.D. in Educational Psychology and Special Education at the University of California, Los Angeles (UCLA), and later completed a postdoctoral fellowship at the Laboratory of Comparative Human Cognition at the University of California at San Diego. His research focuses on sociocultural influences on teaching/learning processes specifically related to academic achievement (especially reading) in at-risk and language minority students and students with learning disabilities; children's acquisition and uses of literacy; and the assessment of learning and achievement.

Grace Zamora-Durán

GRACE ZAMORA-DURÁN is Assistant Executive Director with The Council for Exceptional Children (CEC). She received her doctorate at the University of Arizona in Tucson where she researched the characteristics and educational experiences of students with limited English proficiency who were identified as learning disabled. Her interests continue to be second language learning issues and distinguishing between differences and disabilities among culturally diverse students. Previous to her present position with CEC, Dr. Zamora-Durán worked as a school administrator and an educator in general and special education programs.

CEC Teacher Resources

Reducing Disproportionate Representation of Culturally Diverse Students in Special and Gifted Education *Edited by Alfredo J. Artiles and Grace Zamora-Durán*
Provides new perspectives for working with children from different cultural backgrounds. Suggests alternative ways to assess and teach culturally diverse students who have behavioral problems, other disabilities, and those who are gifted.

      No. P5219, 1997, 104pp.   ISBN 0-86586-297-4
      Regular Price $26.95   CEC Member Price $18.95

Disruption, Disaster, and Death: Helping Students Deal with Crises
by Festus E. Obiakor, Teresa A. Mehring, and John O. Schwenn
This one-of-a-kind resource leads the way in providing a candid look at the problems related to situations that involve disruption, disaster, and death and offers a wide array of resources and practices to help students cope with these events. The content is appropriate for general education, but the book also contains sections on how children with exceptionalities may be specifically affected.

      No. P5190, 1997, 120 pp.   ISBN 0-86586-289-3
      Regular Price $26.95   CEC Member Price $18.95

Crossover Children: A Sourcebook for Helping Children Who Are Gifted and Learning Disabled, Second Edition *by Marlene Bireley*
A rich resource that provides specific strategies to help children who are gifted and learning disabled and/or ADD control impulsivity, increase attention, enhance memory, improve social skills, and develop a positive self-concept. It also provides recommendations for academic interventions and enrichment activities.

      No. P5121, 1995, 94pp.   ISBN 0-86586-264-8
      Regular Price $28.00   CEC Member Price $19.60

Back Off, Cool Down, Try Again: Teaching Students How to Control Aggressive Behavior
by Sylvia Rockwell
A vividly descriptive primer on how to nurture the social development of students with aggressive behavior in a classroom setting using the stages of group development as the basis for classroom management. The focus moves from teacher control to control through peer interaction. Strategies for group management, affective and academic instruction, and planning, documentation, and consultation are presented.

      No. P5120, 1995, 144pp.   ISBN 0-86586-263-X
      Regular Price $27.00   CEC Member Price $19.00

Tough to Reach, Tough to Teach: Students with Behavior Problems *by Sylvia Rockwell*
Through the use of anecdotes, the author prepares teachers for the shock of abusive language and hostile behavior in the classroom. This book will allow you to have a plan for meeting the challenges of teaching these students more effective ways to communicate. Provides many practical management strategies for defusing and redirecting disruptive behavior.

      No. P387, 1993, 106pp.   ISBN 0-86586-235-4
      Regular Price $24.00   CEC Member Price $16.80

Assess for Success: Handbook on Transition Assessment *by Patricia L. Sitlington, Deborah A. Neubert, Wynne Begun, Richard C. Lombard, and Pamela J. Leconte*
Helps the IEP team decide what to assess and how assessment data should be collected and used within the context of career development. Case studies illustrate how this concept applies to students with different levels of ability and different career visions. Provides strategies for assessing self-determination skills.

      No. P5155, 1996, 136pp.   ISBN 0-86586-281-8
      Regular Price $30.00   CEC Member Price $21.00

Prices may change without notice. Send orders to: The Council for Exceptional Children, Dept. K70750, 1920 Association Drive, Reston, VA 20191-1589. 1-800-CEC-READ.